Do Border Dream of Sheep?

*Two Puppies Grow Up, One to be a Sheepdog,
the Other a Service Dog*

Carol Lea Benjamin and C. Denise Wall

Photographs by C. Denise Wall, Carol Lea Benjamin, Stephen
Lennard, Christine Henry, Robin French, and Zachary Joubert.
Wolf photographs by Monty Sloan and Denise Wall
Illustrations by Carol Lea Benjamin

OUTRUN PRESS

ISBN-13: 978-0-9794690-8-4
ISBN-10: 0-9794690-8-2

Library of Congress Control Number: 2010916399

Dedication

For Stephen, my sweetheart,
and for Sky.

For my wonderful husband and daughter, Jim and Erin.
And, of course, for May.

About the Authors

Carol Lea Benjamin is the award-winning author of nine books about dog behavior and training, including *Mother Knows Best, Second-Hand Dog* and *Dog Training in Ten Minutes*, as well as the Shamus-Award winning Rachel Alexander and Dash mystery series. She has been awarded the Dog Writers of America's highest honor, The Distinguished Service Award for Extraordinary Achievement and Communications Excellence, and in 2003, she was elected to the Hall of Fame of the International Association of Canine Professionals for "a lifetime of dedication to dogs and their training." Carol's border collie, Sky, is her fourth service dog.

Denise Wall breeds and trains working border collies and has successfully competed with them at the highest level in sheepdog trials. She has a Ph.D. in biochemistry and currently serves on the Health and Genetics Committee for the American Border Collie Association, the registry for working border collies. She has also served on the Board of Directors for this large, independent dog registry. In addition to scientific writing, Denise is an award-winning photographer whose photos have appeared in many publications, and a videographer. Her popular CDs and DVDs cover all aspects of sheepdog training.

Contents

1

How the Wolf Became the Dog

This is the true story of two border collies who were born on a small farm in North Carolina, both destined to become working dogs. One would remain on the farm to work sheep, like her parents, her grandparents, and all her ancestors before her. The other would become a service dog, a dog who helps a person with a disability, in one of the biggest, busiest cities in the world. Herding is one of the oldest partnerships between human beings and dogs; service work is one of the most recent. Yet both dogs would need to employ instincts from their wild ancestors in order to succeed at their work. So this is a very modern tale that reaches way back in time.

Before the dog, there was the wolf.

Except for their tracks in the snow or in the muddy earth beside a stream, wolves were rarely seen by our earliest ancestors, but in the dead quiet of the night, the eerie sound of their howling might have echoed off the cold stone walls of what was then human housing. For safety's

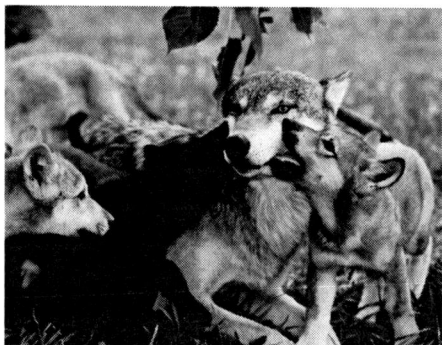

sake, the wolves kept largely to themselves. Others of their own kind were seen as competition for territory and the prey that could be found there. Those who were different were potential meals. What was safe was what was familiar, what was family.

Wolf packs were, in fact, extended families, a male and female and their offspring. When the pups matured, some stayed with the pack, while others, more than likely the boldest ones, left to form packs of their own. Sometimes an outsider would show up, some wolf who'd left another pack. In that case, the wolves might chase him off, or if he was persistent enough not to leave, they might kill him. Occasionally the pack would accept a stranger. This was a double-edged sword. With more wolves to cooperate in the hunt, the pack might be more successful. But in lean times, there would not be enough game to feed a larger family. So it was usually only the alpha or dominant pair who bred. They were the strongest and the wisest of the pack, the best genetic specimens, so their pups would have the best chance of thriving. Life was harsh and life expectancy was short. Population control helped ensure the pack would go on. In the wild, everything is about survival. Toward that end, the dominant pair kept the peace, made safety a priority and led the hunt. They set the mood, initiated all the important activities, and, along with the other adult members of the pack, protected the pups from danger, provided them with food, and taught them the skills they needed in order to survive.

Wolves have no sophisticated verbal or written language like the kind humans eventually developed. Instead, they use a complex system of body language to communicate with each other. They understand the smallest gestures, facial expressions, postures, even ear and tail positions. It is body language that gives the wolves the clues they need to navigate their world, helping them understand other individuals within the pack and also those outside the pack, other wolves who might invade their territory and the prey animals they are hunting.

Their keen senses are part of their efficient and effective system of communication and also help them survive. They can hear each other howling from several miles away, can spot movement at great distances, can see better in the dark than we humans can and their sense of smell is about one hundred times more sensitive than ours.

All the wolves' skills and senses come into play when they hunt for food. Their excitation is palpable and while an observer might not be able to discern how they know the intentions and plans of the others in their pack, they work almost as if they are one being, staying focused on their goal and working as a team until the hunt is over.

When the wolves spot a herd of prey animals, they stalk the herd, circle it and finally get all the animals running.

With the herd on the move, the wolves are able to make an educated guess as to which animal to single out, which one they would have the best chance of catching. Often, but not always, it is one that is weak in some way, very young, old, slow, sick, or lame.

After the wolves separate an animal from the herd, they might surround it. For a moment, predators and prey freeze. No one moves while they assess each other, looking for strengths and weaknesses that will help each side determine how to proceed. The prey animal might take off, running for his life. Or he might hold his ground, deciding to fight instead of fleeing. The wolves might close in, or, feeling the strength and determination of the prey animal, they might leave, hoping for better luck next time around.

No matter how well the wolves cooperate with each other or how hard they work, the hunt is not always successful. When the wolves fail to bring down prey, they go hungry. When the hunt goes well, the wolves share a much-needed meal, gorging themselves in part because wolves in the wild can never be sure when the next meal will be, in part because often there are hungry pups waiting at home.

As soon as the adults get back to the den, the pups mob them, jumping up and licking at their mouths. This triggers the grown-ups to regurgitate some of what they have eaten, giving the pups a feast of their own.

Once the pups are old enough to play, they begin to hone the skills that will help them to be successful when they mature enough to join in on the hunt. They hide and stalk, pounce and chase, and even jump on top of each other, growling and biting. It all looks very fierce, but if they are too rough with a littermate, the game will end. If they are too rough with an adult, they will be corrected, flipped suddenly onto their backs time and again until they learn to inhibit their bite and understand the difference between their relatives and a nice, hot meal.

During play, the pups learn how to assess their own strength, both physical and mental. This lets them know their place in the hierarchy of the pack and even which pup might grow up to leave and become the leader of his own extended family. But these daily skirmishes aren't war. They are rituals, set ways of responding that help keep the peace and prevent the wolves, both young and old, from harming each other. Knowing who is in charge and where they each stand reduces stress for the wolves, replacing it with clarity and peace of mind.

No one knows exactly how the wild wolf gave rise to the domestic dog. It's possible that wolves began to hang around groups of humans because eating their leftovers was a lot easier and a lot safer than hunting large, wild animals that sometimes fought back and injured or killed the wolves who were hunting them. More than likely, it would have been the mildest, friendliest wolves who chose to live near our human ancestors. Since only the tamest of these tamer wolves would have the most success living near people, this selection process helped each generation to be even friendlier and less fearful of humans than the previous ones. As time passed, the relationship with each other was bound to change both species because it wasn't only the wolves who would see an opportunity in living near people. The humans would also see benefits in living near the wolves. The friendliest of the wolf cubs would have made cute pets for the children. As the wolves grew up, they would have helped to protect the den, just as they did when their den had been full of wolves. When they accompanied the humans on the hunt, their superior sense of smell would have helped the humans find the game they were after. And the wolves, even as they became tamer, could circle the prey and keep it from running away, helping their human partners obtain food, an urgent and difficult part of surviving for humans, too, back then.

Selection for tameness not only brought with it changes in behavior—seeking humans rather than fearing them—it brought physical changes as well. Their coloring changed, their ears sometimes flopped down, and they began to vocalize more like the dogs we know today and less like their ancestors. Even their instincts and skills began to change. As dogs took on different jobs, and best worker was bred to best worker, dogs became specialists. The skills needed for each task would become stronger and the skills not useful, and therefore not bred for, would become weaker. Hunting dogs would find the game, but they would leave it up to their human partners to make the kill. When they retrieved the game, instead of making the bird their own lunch, they would deliver it gently to their master. Instead of hunting for their meals, they were now dependent on humans for their food and bringing in the game was part of a job, not a basic means of survival. More and more, their survival relied on their relationship with people. But the wolves, even as they changed, still had an inborn need for leadership and structure. Living with humans, it would be only natural for them to come to see people as their leaders and to work alongside them, take care of them and be taken care of by them, just as they did when their pack consisted only of wolves.

Wolves are social with their own kind, but the new subspecies, the dog, socialized not only with other dogs, but with our species as well. Early on, dogs became more than hunting companions, foot warmers and a primitive but effective early alarm system. They became humankind's best friends.

As their relationship with humans caused the wolf to become the dog, we changed, too. For the first time, we had companionship and assistance not only from our own but also from another species. It's quite possible that, living with dogs, we learned how to appreciate creatures who were different from us, that we stayed in touch with nature, learned new ways to be cooperative, paid more attention to body language, scents and sounds and perhaps, above all, moods. Dogs also brought a different kind of energy into our lives as well as an easy sense of joy, as they still do today. And perhaps it was they who taught us to be more gentle, nurturing and loving. However we changed each other, something clicked, because here we are, still together after all these years.

As we humans continued to breed dogs to each other who excelled at particular jobs, their appearances changed and different breeds emerged. Over time, we molded the subspecies dog into the most diverse creatures on our planet: friends, companions and cohabiters who would ply their inborn skills at a wide variety of jobs in order that both our species could be successful.

This is the story of two such working dogs, of how two sisters grew up and into their jobs and became very different and yet stayed very much the same. This is the story of May and Sky.

2

§ Denise §

Our Puppies Are Born

I breed and train border collies for their original purpose of helping manage livestock on a farm. On my small sheep farm, the border collies help me by doing jobs such as gathering all the sheep from the field and bringing them to the barn. Once the sheep are close, the dogs may then help me by holding them away while I put feed out or hold one or more sheep in place while I medicate, vaccinate, worm, trim hooves or hold new moms with their lambs. Depending on the time of year, the amount and type of work I need them for varies. Even with all the modern advances in technology, there are still many areas of managing livestock that would be very difficult without the help of the collies.

I also go to sheepdog trials, which are competitions where the teamwork and skills of working dogs and their handlers are tested on a specified course. Each phase of the trial is designed to represent some aspect of real work situations. The idea is to "level the playing field" so that dogs and their handlers can be judged on the same field with similar sheep to see which is the best dog/handler team that day of competition in that situation. Trials were originally devised to help shepherds pick the best breeding dogs, so when I go, I not only get to see how well my own dogs are doing, but I also get to see how other dogs are working as well.

Every few years, I need a young dog to train so that my older dogs can retire. When that time came in 2006, I decided my dog, Kate, had proven herself useful and I wanted a puppy from her. Kate is of my breeding and so was her mother, Molly. Kate's relatives have consistently produced sound, healthy pups with a strong desire to herd sheep, and, also very important, the desire to work in partnership with people.

Like many of her relatives, Kate demonstrated through years of sheep work that she had the characteristics that made her worthy to breed. Her greatest strengths are her amazing athletic ability, stamina, and toughness under difficult working situations such as handling stubborn or aggressive sheep.

Aside from working talent, it's important to me to have dogs with good temperaments. Fortunately, Kate is friendly with other dogs and people, and adjusts easily to new situations. She's also quite a character and very playful when not working. She has what in a person would be called a good personality. She seems to understand how to get attention from other dogs and how to make people laugh. Although Kate can be a real ham when she gets around people and dogs, she also plays happily by herself— throwing toys, balls, or whatever she can find in the air, catching them and letting them fall, only

to pounce and fling them in the air again and again. Kate has the most joyful spirit of any dog I've ever had.

Scott, the dog I picked to be the sire of Kate's puppies, is also a good worker who was bred from dogs I knew for several generations. His father's mother, Nan, was a well-known champion sheepdog both in the United States and overseas in the United Kingdom, where the first border collies were bred to work the vast numbers of sheep so important to the economy of that area. Aside from being a great working dog, Nan was known for her ability to sooth not only sheep, but other animals as well.

Like Kate, Scott is healthy and has a friendly, unflappable temperament. He's a bit of a character himself, with his own funny, clownish ways of endearing himself to both people and other dogs. One of his antics is to play bow with the front end of his body on the ground and his rear in the air, and "talk." He has quite a vocal range, so the noises he makes sound almost like words. He seems pleased when he makes people laugh at his goofy ways.

Scott is generally a calmer dog around the house than Kate, who, like many border collies, often finds the "couch potato" lifestyle difficult. Finally, and most important, Scott's style working sheep complements Kate's very well. I felt the two of them would produce healthy, well-rounded puppies with good working ability.

After I was sure Kate was going to have puppies, I made a "whelping box" for her: a safe, secure box for her to have the puppies in. I put this box in the laundry room, which is right off the kitchen, so we could keep a close eye on her. Kate slept in the whelping box for several weeks ahead of time so that she would be comfortable enough to have her puppies in there. Getting Kate to accept my choice of where she was to have the pups was a very important step. Too often, a female will disappear when it's time to deliver her pups. Later, her anxious owner has to search for her and might find mother and puppies someplace odd, like an underwear drawer or out in the woods in a dug-out under a tree root. Fortunately for me, Kate was happy to have her pups in the very same room where she herself had been born years earlier.

Kate's puppies were due on Saturday, November 25th. However, on Thursday, November 23rd, Thanksgiving morning, it was clear she was getting ready to whelp. By 7 A.M. Kate was busily tearing up the newspapers in her whelping box, making her "nest." Because it was Thanksgiving, and because I hadn't expected the puppies for a couple more days, we had planned the traditional Thanksgiving dinner, along with other family members as guests. The table was set in the dining room and the scent of roasting turkey perfumed the house. Soon people would start to arrive with homemade pies, chocolates, and funny stories to tell as we ate our feast. But the laundry room where Kate was in her whelping box is right next to the kitchen, and as soon as the commotion started, with several people cooking at once, Kate got very quiet and seemed not to want to have her puppies. In the wild, having puppies during times of unusual noise and activity could mean a threat to the puppies' lives. By holding off on having the puppies until things were calmer, Kate was probably responding to wolf survival instincts still present in dogs.

So I waited and waited and waited by Kate's side to reassure her, smelling all the delicious food being prepared and hoping Kate would have her puppies before everyone sat down to eat dinner. Hours went by, but Kate's instincts to protect her unborn puppies from harm in the outside world kept her from delivering them until everything was quiet. Sure enough, things got calm at 1 P.M., the precise second I sat down for Thanksgiving dinner. Right as I started to reach for my favorite dish, I heard Kate make a noise, so I went to check on her. It was finally happening. A mostly black female puppy with some white and tan, called tri-colored, was being born.

So that year, Thanksgiving dinner went on without me. But there was no way I'd leave Kate alone at a time like this. After awhile, my husband, Jim, brought me a plate of food and I ate it right where I was, on the floor of the laundry room, next to Kate. She had five more puppies, a new one every hour or so. Even as a first-time mother, she instinctively knew what to do as each pup was born. She carefully licked each one clean and guided it to a nipple with the others where it could get its first drink of milk. She didn't need any help from me, but I think she was happy to have me with her for support. I kept other people and dogs from disturbing her so she would feel things were quiet enough to continue having the puppies. By that evening, she had six healthy puppies, four girls and two boys. When the pups are first born, it's not always easy to tell if they are black and white or if they will also develop some tan or brown on them as they grow up. A quick peek under their tail will show the first indications of any tan that will show up later. As it turned out, both boys and two of the girls would be tri-colored. The remaining two females were black and white.

Puppies cannot see or hear for a couple of weeks after they're born. For the first few days, they're pretty much just little eating and sleeping machines. From the beginning, they are also little heat-seeking missiles. They seek comfort, warmth, and food by sensing the body heat of the other puppies and mom and moving toward it. This is how they find the

nipples to drink milk. They nurse until they fall asleep and roll away, sometimes with their mouth still shaped like it's around a nipple.

In fact, at this stage of their lives, everything appears to be a nipple.

Even when they're still very young, puppies have experiences that will shape their future personalities and temperament. They are influenced by such things as how well the mother cares for them, if they get enough to eat, if they're warm enough, and how much they're touched by the other puppies, the mother, and people. Fortunately, Kate's litter was in a warm, comfortable place in the laundry room and she had plenty of food to produce enough milk for all the puppies. Unlike wolf pups in the wild, Kate and her puppies did not have to fight for survival. However, some stress helps stimulate the puppies' brains to grow and develop to their fullest potential. Kate stimulated them by nuzzling and licking each of them frequently as a good mother should. There were enough of them so that each puppy was able to cuddle with littermates but also had to fight to get the nipple with the most milk.

Newborn puppies shouldn't be constantly handled, but some handling by people will help them become accustomed to new experiences as they grow up. Unlike wolf pups in the wild, our puppies' social development needed to include building a strong bond with humans from the very beginning. Every day members of our family took each of the puppies out of the whelping box and spent some time holding, stroking, cuddling, and, later, playing with them. Having a litter of pups is a special time for our family. We don't have pups very often, and when we do, we enjoy each minute spent with them. Early on, when they spent most of their time nursing, my husband would put one on his chest or cuddle it beside him as he was lying on the couch watching TV. After awhile, the puppy would get hungry and need to go back to the nursing group. My husband would say, "Pop me off a fresh one. This one's ready to go back." And so it went all evening. As one pup got hungry, I would go detach another nursing puppy from Kate's nipple to bring to Jim to cuddle until he had cycled through them all.

My daughter, Erin, enjoyed putting the pups on the carpeted floor and letting them crawl around and find her again. As for me, well, I can only have pups every few years because I basically don't get much else done when I have puppies. My favorite thing is to sit in the whelping box or puppy pen for hours and let the pups crawl all over me—

mouthing, tugging my clothes, playing and finally sleeping like a blanket of puppies all over me. So as it turned out, each person in our family had a different role in socializing the pups. Erin liked to interact and play with them, initiating activity. Jim liked to cuddle and let them sleep beside him. Because I had more time, I did everything, but mostly let them interact with me. Much like the wolf packs, each member of our human family had a special role in the raising of the pups.

Also like the wolf packs in the wild, some of our family dogs took on individual roles in helping raise the pups, too. Not all dogs like puppies; my older males, Mick and Todd, didn't want to have much to do with them, so we didn't let them out when the pups were out. But Molly, the pups' grandmother, seemed to understand her role in nurturing them, especially during the times when Kate was spending less time with them. Molly had no milk, so the puppies didn't pester her to nurse like they did Kate. Instead, she provided affection, indulgence, and occasional guidance in how to behave, giving them a chance to interact with a receptive adult dog other than their mom. Another of my dogs, Zeke, enjoyed playing with the pups, much like Erin. He was very gentle with them, mouthing them in play and rolling around with them but never being too rough for the pup's age.

The adult dogs in the household that interacted with the pups amazingly let the pups do all sorts of things they would never let another adult dog do—jump on them, steal their food or treats, and chew or pull on them. We call this a "puppy license." It allows the puppies to do things early on that the adult dogs would never tolerate from an adolescent dog. Even though it's just a game, playing at being insubordinate helps the puppies build enough confidence to try new things, or later on, to challenge the leaders for the top position in the pack. When the pups are a little older, but before they leave the farm, Kate will

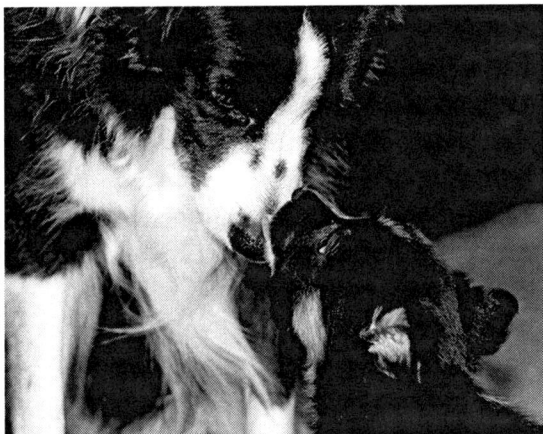

temper their bratty behavior so that they don't get into too much trouble once they are out among strange dogs. These interactions with both humans and other dogs are important for normal social development. Growing up well rounded is a lot of work for the puppies, the mother, the people taking care of them, and even the other dogs in the family.

Puppies' eyes start to open at about ten days. They begin to hear as their ears open at around three weeks. Even before their eyes and ears are open, they start making little grunting noises and mouthing each other. Before long, they are play-fighting, growling fiercely, tussling, chasing each other and rolling around.

Differences in puppies start to show up very early on. Some fight harder to get the nipples with the most milk. Some seem calmer or sleep more than others. Some appear to like being handled more than others. Some make more noise than others. As the puppies interact more and more with each other, the role of the mother becomes less for a time. When this time came in Kate's litter, she began to leave the puppies for short periods. She returned to feed and clean the pups, and in general make sure things were going well. As the puppies became stronger, it took less time for them to eat, and they had more time for play. But like the wolf pups, what looks like play is really a way for them to sort out which puppies are the strongest and might make the best leaders. It is a way for them to find their place in the group so they can feel secure. These are the beginnings of learning the social skills they will need to get along with other dogs as they mature.

It's difficult to know for sure what a puppy's personality will be like when it grows up. Still, I watched Kate's pups carefully for clues from the very first day. I tried to build a picture in my mind of what each puppy might be like when it grew up. The puppy buyers had all agreed to let me pick the puppy that I felt would best suit them, and I already knew what kind of personality would be right for each. So I started trying to figure out which puppy would be best for each home from the very beginning. Although border collies are best known for their herding ability, a well-bred collie can do other jobs. One of Kate's pups was destined to be a service dog. I watched closely for any signs of a pup that seemed especially empathetic, full of feeling for others. The first born puppy, the one who would later be named Sky, appeared to be unusually cuddly, even when she was only a few days old. If we put her on the carpet in the den by herself a few feet away, her heat-seeking instinct would help her find her way back to us. If your hand was open near her, she would find it and curl into your palm as if she were trying to touch and press against as much of you as possible. All of the pups would seek the heat of our bodies or each other when placed alone like this, but little Sky seemed more comforted and content curled up against us in this way than the others.

There was another thing Sky did that really stood out to me. Another puppy, Moss, was much more verbal than the others from the time he was born. He was not sick or hungry; he was simply the most vocal of the pups. If there was a puppy making lots of noise, it was usually him.

He would some-
times wake up away
from the other pups
and cry helplessly,
and quite loudly. On
one occasion when
he did this, Sky, who
was peacefully
sleeping piled up
with the other pups,
got up and crawled
over to the scream-
ing puppy. She curled
up beside Moss,
snuggling up

against him as closely as possible. In no time, noisy Moss
became quiet and fell asleep. The pups could hear by this
point, so in my mind it would not have been pleasant to go
plop down beside that screaming puppy. I could hardly
believe what I had just seen. I thought it was a very
significant thing for Sky to do. Along with her desire to
cuddle, she seemed to have some inborn desire to comfort
others. The natural desire to be very close to and comfort
others is a good trait for a potential service dog.

Another of the females was more feisty and independent than the others. I was going to keep a female puppy from the litter for myself, and this is exactly the type of dog I like to work sheep with. As her independent nature emerged, I began to watch her more closely as my possible pick. Our family had decided ahead of time we would keep a female and name her May, after a dog in her great grandmother's pedigree. As we watched this feisty pup grow, and began to feel she might be our pick, we nicknamed her "Maybe" as a joke. However, as with all the pups, the process in my mind to choose which pup would best fit each home included everything I observed about each pup over time. I didn't make the final decision until the pups were five weeks old.

At about three weeks, because they're not very steady on their legs yet, pups start to do something that like looks like they're half crawling and half walking. When Kate's pups got to this age, I began feeding them goat's milk mixed with softened kibble. At first it was a big mess with more food getting on the pups than in them. They wanted to eat, but fell into the bowl over and over, teetering either too far away or completely submerged in the sloppy mix, stumbling into the bowl and sneezing food out all over each other and the room.

After those first meals there was quite a mess with wet, kibble-colored puppies wearing food from mouth to tail. Kate especially enjoyed this time, cleaning the food off their mouths, faces, feet, and even bellies after their meals. They also enjoyed cleaning each other off. After they finished licking each other, their mouthings turned into tousling and play fighting.

Finally, the full, satisfied and exhausted pups would fall asleep.

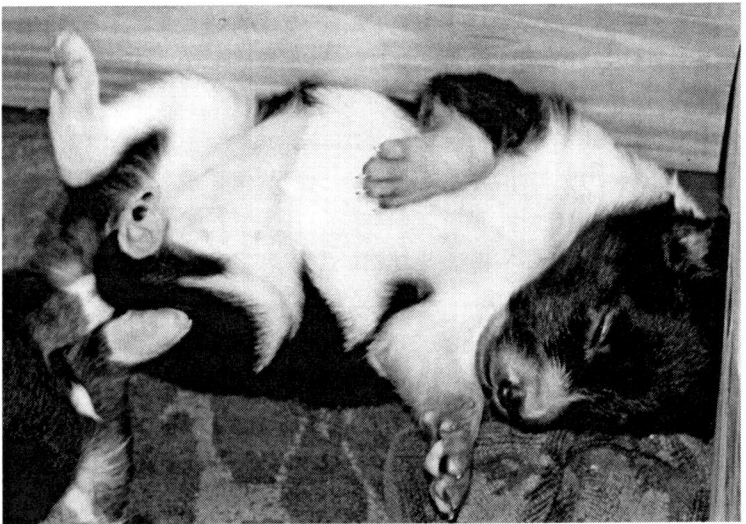

In a few days, they were able to eat very efficiently. They dove into the food and grunted like little pigs, pushing each other and the bowls around on the floor as they each struggled to get the most.

As they ate more of this goat's milk kibble mixture, they needed to nurse from Kate less and less. By about five weeks, they were only nursing two or three times a day and well on their way to not needing food from Kate anymore.

When things got a little less messy, feeding time became a great time for the family to interact with the pups. I remember the Christmas morning, after the pups had eaten, our whole family sat on the floor in the kitchen with all of them. At four weeks old, they were coordinated enough to run a little and so we became human pieces of the gymnasium of fun they were discovering in the house. They ran and jumped on and played with each other and us until they couldn't go anymore. Then they all found a place on a lap to crawl up on and sleep. It was a great way to start Christmas day.

By the time the puppies were about three weeks old, it was the dead of winter. However, we were blessed with a few good days warm enough that I could take the pups outside for a few minutes at a time. I waited until they had eaten and were awake so they would be comfortable and ready for a new experience. At first I took them out and put them in the grass two at a time. I stayed very close, but let them crawl around, come back to me, or cuddle together. I watched each pup for their reaction to the sights, sounds, and feel of the outside. The first time they all mostly explored very briefly and then wanted to come back to me or to the other puppy. Some of them whined or cried when they'd had enough. The first sessions outside were very short. Eventually, as they became more used it, I took the puppies out one at a time. Both "Maybe" and Sky seemed overall very confident in the new situation from the very first session.

Naturally, the people waiting for puppies were dying to know which one would be theirs. When the pups were about five weeks old, I made my final choices. My initial impression of the feistiest girl held up over time and the pup we had been calling "Maybe" became simply our May.

That afternoon, I wrote everyone else. The smallest pup, Sky, would be going to New York City to become a service dog. The rest of the pups, two boys, Moss and Sweep, and two girls, Leia and Eve, were all going to learn sheep herding. Moss, Sweep, and Leia would live nearby

and May and I would be able to visit them. Eve, like Sky, would be flying to her new home. She would be going all the way to Arizona.

All of Kate's puppies, with the exception of Leia, had been given one-syllable names. Unlike many other breeds, working border collies are traditionally given short, simple names such as Meg, Nell, Fly, and Jess for females and Ben, Moss, Roy, and Cap for males. The reason for this is that it's easier and faster for the shepherd in a work situation to say these simple names and easier for the dog to understand that you mean him or her. Another tradition is that many working border collie pups are named after admirable dogs in their pedigrees, as we had done with May. So peculiar as it seems, there are many, many working border collies with the same exact names.

Once I had decided which puppy would go to whom, I started tailoring their experiences in small ways to help suit their new homes and environments. Carol's pup, Sky, would be living in a big noisy city. As a little puppy, it might be somewhat overwhelming for her. Because of this, I tried to find ways to help her cope and find comfort until she became bigger and more used to the noise. When I walked the adult dogs in the field for exercise each day, I nestled Sky in my coat and zipped it up so her head was showing and she could see things, but her body was cradled and held in by the waistband of my coat. There was enough room that she could retreat almost completely into the comfort of my coat and still breathe if there were too much noise or activity for her. I did this "coat cuddling" on walks with all of the pups to some degree on a rotating basis, but I wanted to make sure Sky in particular was comfortable with this natural and comforting way to avoid becoming overwhelmed in the airport and once she got to New York.

By four weeks of age, the pups were already running around together inside the house. By the time they were five weeks old, they were quite feisty in the house. I could only let them out one at a time or in groups of two or three so that I could keep track of them. Sometimes they'd tussle around on the carpet in the den or tear through the house chasing each other or play tug-of-war with a toy. I loved to watch their antics as they ran around in the house. Best of all, I loved to watch them play with Molly, their grandmother. Playing inside was fun for them and running on different surfaces would help them when they got out into the world. But whenever they got to go outside, they really cut lose. It was winter, and often cold, and at first, some of them seemed glued to one spot or each other. But soon enough, they were running around, climbing the porch steps, chasing each other, exploring the mulch pile, and wrestling on the cold grass. When one of the pups seemed cold, I'd pick it up and let it warm up inside my jacket. Sometimes, once the pup got warm, it would fall asleep. Most often, it would be wiggling around, ready to go back down on the ground to play.

Other things I did to prepare the pups for their new lives included taking them for car rides—several short rides, and one long one that lasted two hours. I also began separating each one from the rest of their littermates for short periods of time. It would be stressful for the pups to be separated from their littermates and the only home they knew to go to a new home. I wanted to introduce them to things they would have to deal with as much as possible to ease their transition.

Hard as it is, all babies need to grow up and leave mom eventually. I try to let weaning be as natural as possible by letting the mother decide when the puppies need to stop expecting milk from her. By six weeks, the puppies were eating enough food that they really didn't need Kate to feed them any longer. By then, especially since they now had sharp little teeth, she was ready to stop nursing them. Her attempts to dissuade them from nursing were interesting. She was very patient and gentle trying to draw them into play rather than nursing. She would sometimes just run off. As they caught on and got faster, this strategy worked less well so she would whirl around and try to engage them in other activities by play bowing and pouncing around.

Once the pups were mostly weaned, Kate was able to take on a larger role in teaching them all sorts of things that would be useful to them for the rest of their lives. Moms all handle this phase differently. Kate remained very interactive, taking quite a bit of time showing the pups how to behave and submit to elders. When teaching the pups, the mothers usually pick the most dominant pup and continually make that pup submit to them by putting their mouth around the pup's neck and pinning it gently on the ground until the pup signals it will not fight her anymore.

Out of this litter, Kate apparently picked Moss as the most dominant puppy to teach submission. It was this puppy that she targeted ninety percent of the time to run after, catch and hold down. Moss must have been very persistent in not learning what Kate was trying to teach him, because he was constantly being run down and pinned.

Occasionally she would pin one of the other puppies just to make sure they, too, got the message. Whenever a pup got pinned, the other pups looked on and learned how to behave.

Eventually, all she needed to do for most of the puppies was to turn and look at them to make them lie down or roll over on their backs in submission.

This is all part of the process of weaning and teaching them she was in charge. Kate is a playful, confident dog who naturally became a loving, careful mother and a gentle, yet firm teacher. Whether she was letting them nurse, one more time, or gracefully dodging them, turning things into a game instead of a meal, she was always interesting and fun to watch as she carried out the inborn socialization rituals performed by wolves and now dogs for thousands and thousands of years.

When the puppies got to be seven weeks old, some of them were ready to go to their new homes. Leia left first, followed a day later by Moss and Sweep. With Moss gone, Kate chose the most dominant female left to show her how to behave. Not surprisingly, this female was the feisty May, the puppy I had chosen to keep.

The remaining three pups would stay together until eight weeks of age. I spent some time each day making sure Sky and Eve had additional experience riding in a car, going places with lots of people and confusion like the feed store, and using the bathroom on "puppy pads" in case they needed to go on them if the flight was long or delayed. Both seemed to take the new experiences in stride. I was a little fretful about their flights, but both would ride in the passenger area along with the new owners, and I felt as if they were prepared as much as possible.

I was happy to have those few extra days with Sky and Eve, but I was also looking forward to being able to concentrate on May, to the time when she would be the only puppy on the farm and we could start our lives together.

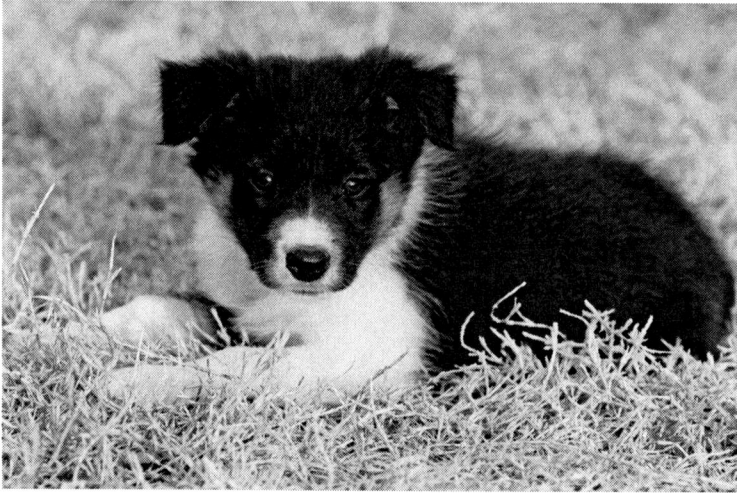

3

§ Carol §

City Dog

My service dog, Flash, was already ten, no longer young in dog years, and though he loved taking care of me, it was getting to be too stressful for him.

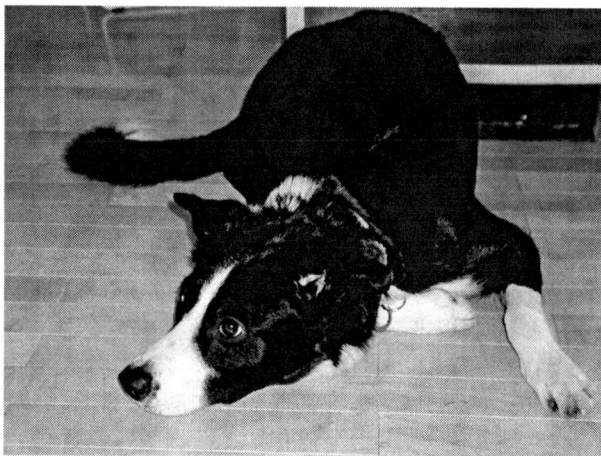

I needed to find and raise a new pup who would take over some of the work so that Flash could have a break, and eventually, let the pup take care of me when he no longer could do it himself, but I kept delaying. Though Flash would always stay with me, I couldn't bear the idea of some other dog taking over his job. I knew it was necessary because dogs age at a faster rate than humans. There'd been another service dog before Flash, my dog, Dexter, who had retired and lived the rest of his life at home being pampered and loved by his family and friends. But, still, the transition is always so difficult. Finally, when I could no longer deny what I knew to be true, that Flash absolutely needed help with his job, I began to search for a female pup, a well-bred working border collie that would be able to do the job when she grew up.

A friend of mine knew a good breeder of working collies, Denise Wall, and said that while she didn't breed often, she was about to breed her dog, Kate. She wrote Denise and told her I needed a young collie to raise and train to be a service dog, so before I even wrote Denise myself, she knew that I could give a useful job and a good home to one of her pups.

Shortly after that, Denise and I began e-mailing back and forth about our dogs and the work they did. We sent pictures, too, so before my puppy was born, I'd seen her mother, her father, her grandparents, and her half-uncle working and playing and Denise had seen what Flash's life was like in New York.

By the time the puppies were born, Flash had had another birthday—he was eleven. Now the need for another dog was even more pressing. When Denise started sending puppy pictures, any remaining hesitation disappeared. In fact, I immediately fell in love—with all of them. They were the most adorable little creatures I had ever seen.

Denise said that all the puppy buyers had agreed to let her pick the right puppy for each of them. I said that was fine with me, too. After all, she would know them better than any of us would. In order to choose a puppy who might have the special ability to become a service dog, she asked me to tell her more about what the dog would do for me.

It's always been very difficult for me to talk about my illness. When I first got it, the doctors told me it was my fault, which was the thinking years ago about many illnesses. Telling people about it made me feel terrible. Even though I now know the truth, that it's not my fault, I still needed an easy way to tell Denise how and why a dog could help me. So I let pictures do some of the talking for me.

§§§

I use a service dog to help me with Crohn's disease, a chronic illness that causes inflammation of the digestive tract, diarrhea, and severe pain. My dog's job is to figure out when I'm pain, where the pain is and what to do about it, all on his own.

It's natural for dogs to comfort each other with the warmth of their bodies. They often do the same for us, especially if we are sick or hurting.

I chose a border collie for the job because they have the ability to focus intensely on the job at hand, they have a strong desire to work with a human partner, and they are highly intelligent.

Border collies are also very active, which makes them cheerful to be around,

and very reactive, which means they notice every little thing.

The dog's desire to help comes from being with his partner 24/7.

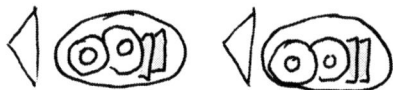

The dog's ability to help comes from his wolf ancestry. If animals that hunt in order to eat couldn't tell which prey animals were sick or weak, they'd starve.

Luckily, dogs view us as pack members. Instead of hunting us down and eating us for lunch, they look for ways to help us, the way wolves in a pack help each other to survive.

The warmth, energy, and pressure of the dog's body against mine helps my body release endorphins, our natural pain killer. Petting a dog helps increase the flow of oxytocin in both humans and dogs. This is the hormone that helps mothers and babies bond with each other. The more powerful the bond, the more the dog wants to help, the more the help he offers works.

When Flash leans tight against me and I stroke his head and back, my body chemistry changes (as does his) and the pain diminishes or disappears.

That's better. I think I'll write a book.

Denise had never chosen a dog to be a service dog before, but she began to tell me that one of the puppies simply exuded sweetness and that she would watch to see if other traits developed as she grew that would make her the right choice for me.

Each week, there would be another story about this one puppy, about how she wiggled and crawled on the rug one day to get to Denise's hand and snuggle inside it, pushing herself against Denise's skin. And about the day that one of the boy pups fell asleep away from the pile of his sleeping littermates and woke up to find himself alone and cold. When he began to cry, it was this same little pup who left the warm pile of puppies to go to him and curl around him, warming him up so that he could go back to sleep. That was exactly the kind of help I needed from a service dog.

The puppies were still so young and were changing every day. Denise didn't reveal which pup she was talking about because she worried that I'd get my heart set on that one and be disappointed if it turned out that she wasn't the right one for me. But I was falling in love anyway. Each week, Denise would e-mail new pictures of the puppies. My husband, Steve, printed the pictures for me and they were framed and placed all around the room in which I write. Each day, I fell in love with a different puppy. Mostly, I liked the ones with interesting markings, the flashier pups, even though I well knew that what you live with is not adorable freckles on a dog's snout or funny markings on its ears, but what the dog is like. It's the dog's character that makes the relationship work. It's who the dog is, not its appearance, that makes the bond between person and dog tight. Still, it's impossible not to fall for a cute puppy. And fall I did, first for one, then the next, then the next.

One day, when the pups were almost five weeks old, I was about to look at the pictures and see who my favorite was that day, but I stopped because something funny occurred to me. Sometimes the very thing you are looking for is right under your nose, but you don't see it. I gathered all the pictures and studied them carefully, looking at each puppy for a long time and then, somehow, I knew which pup would be mine. It was the one I'd never chosen before, the smallest one, the one Denise called the little dark tri.

That very afternoon, Denise told me that the sweet, cuddly dog she had been describing was the little dark tri and asked if I wanted her. I wrote back immediately and said I did, and that I'd decided to call her Sky.

I planned to fly down to North Carolina the day the puppies turned eight weeks of age. Eight weeks is the youngest the airlines allow puppies to fly. Also, between seven and eight weeks of age, puppies are ready and able to bond to their new people and adjust to a new environment.

And what an adjustment Sky would have, moving from a quiet farm to New York City.

I always felt bad taking a puppy from a farm and bringing it to the city with all the traffic and noise and so few opportunities to run off leash. But one night, shortly before I was due to go to Denise's farm and bring Sky home, I got out of a taxi downtown where I would catch the Staten Island Ferry to go and hear a friend's band play. I stood looking up at the tall buildings, the lights sparkling everywhere, the energy of the city just crackling. The city seemed magical and alive and I stood there for a moment unable to move. My dog will have a wonderful life here, I thought, full of important work, adventures, and love. I had my airline tickets already. In a few days, I would be meeting Sky.

There was an ice storm in North Carolina the day of my flight. The roads were slick and as Denise drove slowly and carefully from the airport to her farm, we saw several cars that had skidded onto the shoulder and even a couple that were hanging into the ditch that lined the highway. When we got to the farm, we went right to where the puppies were. One of the girls, Leia, and both boys, Sweep and Moss, had gone off to their new homes earlier that week. Only three girls were there, the one Denise was keeping, called May, the one other pup who was flying to her new home, Eve, and my pup, Sky. They were all adorable, all jumping up and down for attention, but I only saw Sky. From that first moment, I only had eyes for her.

I spent a few hours at the farm with Denise watching Sky play with Molly, her grandmother, and with May and Eve. She was a busy little thing, running all over the house, playing with toys, sometimes taking time out to come to me or to Denise for kisses. Denise had been carrying her around in her jacket to get her used to that, thinking I might need to do that in the airport and, in fact, that's exactly what I ended up doing. I had a Sherpa bag with me, the kind of soft carrying case the airlines require for dogs who are traveling in the cabin, but I didn't want her in it a minute longer than necessary. I thought she'd be happier if she were in my jacket, pressed against my heart, and that I'd be, too.

I worried about going through security with a puppy even though I had all the documents the airline required, but when the head of security saw Sky's face poking out of my jacket, he, too, fell in love. So that part of the trip was a piece of cake. But the flight home turned out to be anything but. My flight was delayed for hours and there I was with an eight week old puppy who needed to eat every few hours and needed to relieve herself even more often. I had a small amount of kibble with me but no dish. After the second delay in my flight was announced, I made a little pile of kibble on the rug in the waiting area and put Sky down next to it. She ate every morsel and looked for more. I also had a couple of Wee-Wee pads with me, in case of emergency. I picked Sky up, took her into the ladies room, spread the Wee-Wee pad out on the floor and told her "Go potty," which Denise had been telling the puppies every time she let them out on the grass. It worked like a charm, letting Sky know that even though this didn't look like the lawn back at the farm, this was the spot to use. By the time we finally boarded our flight to New York, Sky was exhausted. She spent the entire trip sleeping on my jacket on the empty seat next to mine, my hand gently resting on her so she'd know I was there. And perhaps so I'd know she was there.

Across the aisle from us sat a mother and a young girl, about nine. She was tired, too, and slept, like Sky, for most of the trip. But when the plane landed, the little dog and the little girl noticed each other. I held Sky across the aisle and while we taxied to the gate, there were a lot of kisses exchanged. I was thrilled to see my puppy was good with children. Part of my job raising her would be to make sure she could move through the world with ease, that new things wouldn't startle or scare her and that she would find new creatures, both human and canine, as appealing and delightful as she and this little girl found each other. We were off to a perfect beginning.

The next hurdle was introducing Sky to Flash. Normally, this wouldn't be tough. But as Flash got more and more into his job, he became less and less interested in other dogs, and finally, less and less tolerant of them. Dogs he would meet in the street might have seemed silly to him, jumping around and barking, nothing to do but play all day long. Flash had done that, too, for nearly four years, before he became a service dog. And while he still played, it was a good game of fetch that he appreciated. Sometime around the age of five or six, he stopped socializing with other dogs. Now I was going to bring a playful little puppy into his life, and I didn't know how he'd take that. Much as he needed a helper, he would not want to give up his job. He would not want to share me. And perhaps most of all, he would not want a silly puppy in his face demanding that he play.

But Sky had her own ideas.

I didn't bring Sky right into the house. Instead, I called Steve from the lobby of our building and asked him to bring out Flash so that the dogs could meet on neutral territory. Flash's tail went in circles when he saw me. He jumped up to greet me and ignored Sky.

We took them for a short walk and Flash continued to act as if the puppy weren't there. Once inside, I whisked Sky away to the area I had set up for her with a small crate, a newspaper "yard," some dog toys and a bowl of water. I gave her food and a kiss, thinking that she'd settled down there so that I could pay some attention to Flash. We could hear her crunching her kibble. Moments later, she appeared in the living room. I picked her up and brought her back, checking to make sure the barrier I'd carefully set up was secure. A minute later, she was out again. It seemed she was happy to be home and wanted to inspect her new house. That was fine with me, but I didn't know if it would be fine with Flash.

To my utter surprise, Flash didn't seem bothered that this interloper was invading his home. After checking out everything and getting the lay of the land, Sky approached Flash and bowed, inviting him to play. He looked puzzled at first, but Sky would not take no for an answer and that night, the tone of their relationship was established. Sky would let him know when she wanted to play, he would hesitate for a moment, and then he'd give in and the game would be on. In no time at all this bossy little creature had taken over the house. Oddly, none of us seemed to object, not even Flash. He actually seemed happy to have a friend.

Every half hour or so, we opened the door to the garden and took them both out. Sky had no trouble translating the grass at the farm to our paved yard, and house training turned out to be very easy. Not quite as easy was getting her used to the city and its loud and startling noises and strange-looking creatures. On her first walk, the very next day, she met her first city dogs, two dachshunds wearing winter coats. Sky had never seen a dog that wasn't a border collie. And she certainly had never seen a dog wearing clothes. She backed up until she hit my legs, turned and stood up against them, asking to be picked up.

To a wild animal, like a wolf, strange sights and unfamiliar noises mean danger and they will do whatever they can to avoid them. In order to survive, a young wolf must pay attention to his innate fears. He must hide or flee. But dogs are extremely adaptable, all the more so when they are young. In order to survive, a dog must wrap herself around her human family, learning to live where they live and adjusting to their way of doing things, to the noises and sights in their neighborhood, even sometimes, to seeing dogs wearing coats. Unlike wolves, dogs can do this. They can learn to feel at home in an amazing variety of environments and become accustomed to a rich variety of life styles. Dogs thrive wherever there are people, on farms, in cities, in the ice cold north and in the hot and humid south, living and working side by side with humans in any and all conditions.

In order to help Sky adjust, for the first few days I carried her a lot. She'd walk for a minute and then come close and put a paw on my legs, asking to ride in my jacket. Alternating letting her walk and carrying her helped her get used to the strange and loud noises of the city and gave her an escape from the funny-looking dogs in coats that didn't look like dogs to her.

The dog who changed her mind about city dogs was a huge Golden Retriever. His mistress did pet therapy with him, taking him into the hospital to visit patients, so he knew to move slowly and wait for an invitation to come closer. He was the perfect dog to let Sky know that she could play with dogs other than border collies and that city dogs were, by and large, a social lot.

Learning to play with dogs of other breeds meant that Sky had to hone her skills at reading body language. While the basic postures are the same as they are with wolves, domestic dogs have a more varied range of appearance than do wolves, so reading them takes some skill. For example, different breeds have different ear carriage, size and shape, and this can skew the message dogs are reading. When wolves have to know the intent of another wolf, things are clearer. All wolves have mobile, erect ears. So ears forward always mean a dominant stance and ears held back, a submissive one. But with the domesticated dog all ears are not the same. Some are tiny, some face down, some are held close to the head while others seem to fly out to the side. Some dog ears are erect, like wolf ears, and these can be pressed back or held forward to express different emotions, but others, those that are surgically cropped, like the Doberman's ears, tend to stay erect, giving a message of dominance no matter what the dog is feeling.

Even tails can present a problem. Wolves' tails can he held high, straight out, relaxed and downward or, when a wolf is frightened, tucked up against the belly. But some dogs have tails that almost always stay curled. Others have docked tails, tails that have been surgically shortened when the dogs were small pups. This can be very confusing to a dog who isn't used to many breeds. Over time, Sky became keen at reading other dogs accurately and also at "talking" back to them, crouching low when first meeting to indicate that she was friendly and posed no threat. This is the perfect way for strange dogs to signal each other that play would be welcome. By spring, Sky had learned to play with goldens and beagles, spaniels and Labs, poodles and schnoodles, dogs and puppies of every size, shape and color. One day, we met a Chihuahua wearing a frilly pink dress. Sky play bowed and the two girls began a game. Watching them, I knew my puppy had come a long way from the farm.

Of course Sky wasn't only meeting dogs. By the time she'd been in New York City about a month, she'd met and been petted by dozens and dozens of people of all ages, colors, and sizes. Once, when we were out for a walk, a homeless man admired her. Even in his tattered clothes, he seemed dignified, and when he told me how pretty my dog was, his voice was soft and gentle. I'd seen him before, on the block facing the Hudson River. Like many homeless people, he had staked out a place for himself, a cardboard box with some blankets draped over it, and whenever I saw him, there was a bowl of water out and another of food. Like me, he had a dog of his own.

Around that time, I discovered a puppy playgroup. It was nothing formal, just a few dog walkers, a few dog owners, and a few puppies who met every day at noon in a little park not far from where I live. Since I knew socializing Sky was not only important for her well being but also necessary for her future as a service dog, every day I stopped work at a quarter to twelve and headed for Abingdon Square Park, where the puppies met to chew on each other's faces, race in circles, jump, crouch, rest, and start all over again.

At home, Sky and Flash kept inventing new games. Every one had a set of rules that they both understood, but every few days, one or the other would change the rules and the games would become more elaborate and more fun for us to watch. Sky, it seemed, had transformed Flash into what she needed. She had an older dog to copy and cavort with. He had reconnected with his own puppyhood. He had never seemed happier. More than that, Sky was learning by watching Flash. When I taught her to sit on command or lie down or come, Flash would be her model of behavior, showing her, by his example, what the words I was saying meant.

Sky had been in cars a couple of times and in a taxi on the way home from the airport, but even when Flash came along, she wasn't thrilled riding in vehicles, and the sooner I got her past that, the better. I had applied for service dog certification right away, knowing I'd need it in order to teach her the things she had to learn for her future job. I couldn't teach her how to ride on the bus, for example, unless I had the right to take her onto the bus. So she had her service dog tag early, plus a little red cape that said "service dog in training." Like the puppy raisers who help future guide dogs learn to navigate the human world, including going to stores, being polite and quiet in restaurants, going along on visits to the doctor or trips to the supermarket, I was about to take Sky on her first bus ride.

The size of the bus and its slow, lumbering progress meant that Sky would be less likely to get motion sickness than she would in a car. This was a good thing. But the noises a bus makes and the large number of strangers and tight quarters make the ride difficult. I decided on two things.
First, to start, I would carry Sky and keep her on my lap. That was easy because she was still so small, almost too small for the red cape she was wearing.

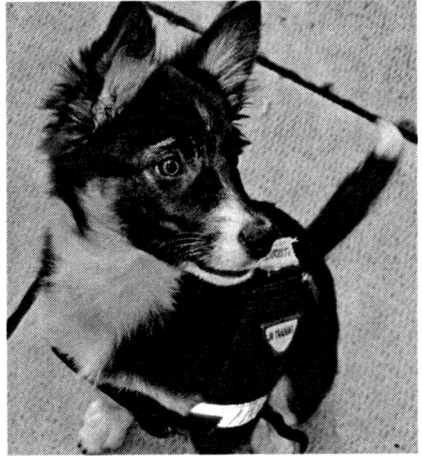

Second, though service dogs should not be distracted when they are working, I decided that if I let every kid on the bus pet Sky, she'd think the bus was a fun place to be. So that's exactly what I did. I got on the bus with her just when school let out and it was filled with kids on their way home. I didn't have to carry her up and down the aisle and ask each kid if they wanted to pet my puppy. They all came to us, crowding around where I sat with Sky on my lap, asking first and then touching her so gently. They wanted to know her name and how old she was. Each time a kid repeated her name, her tail wagged quickly from side to side. She kissed every child who came to pet her until the bus was full of giggles. I couldn't have been more delighted. We rode for about a mile, got off and hiked home. Every time another bus pulled over, Sky was ready to get on board. One ride had her convinced that bus rides were terrific.

Cabs, unfortunately, were not so easy, but since we didn't have a car, we used them often. There were no friendly kids in cabs to distract Sky from the starting and stopping that made her stomach feel all queasy. Even though I had her on my lap and held on tight, sometimes we'd go flying forward and then slide back against the seat. We took short rides at first—just a few blocks—but I could see that Sky was more than relieved to get out each time. She'd pull to get as far away from the cab as she could and each time I stepped off the curb to hail another taxi and try again, she'd pull back from the street and try to escape. When a cab stopped, I'd have to pick her up to get her inside. I worried a lot about this—a service dog needs to be cool about everything, including riding in taxis—but I was unable to come up with a solution for several months.

One day I was busy working at home while Sky and Flash were tearing through the house playing catch-me-if-you-can and suddenly the sound of little feet going from room to room stopped. It was very quiet. Too quiet. I got up from the computer and walked into the living room to a bizarre sight. There was Flash lying down, his chin resting on the rug. Sky was there, too, sitting on Flash's head. It looked as if she'd backed up and sat. I'd never seen anything so silly. It had to be an accident, I thought. She must have been standing in front of him and then decided to sit, not realizing that he was right behind her. But in subsequent days, I found her doing it again and again. To my utter surprise, Flash, the dog who didn't like physical contact with other dogs, seemed perfectly content. Even more ridiculous, one day I met a friend while out on a walk

with Sky. Her dog, a big, old, hairy Old English sheepdog named Toby, jumped around with Sky and then lay down on the sidewalk. Sky backed up, that slow, careful way that trucks back up, and sat down on Toby's head. Like Flash, Toby seemed to think this was a great idea, and the two dogs stayed that way until Sky and I went in one direction and Toby and Judy, his person, headed the other way.

Seeing the world, not just her own house and backyard, was helping Sky build confidence. When dogs see something odd looking that they've never seen before, an overturned trash can or a plastic bag blowing in the wind, it can make them cautious or even fearful. They sometimes stop walking and crouch low with their tails tucked up against their bellies. Whenever this happened, I would encourage Sky to investigate. If possible, I'd tap the object and gently call her over to sniff it. She'd keep her body low and move slowly until she smelled what I was touching. Once she did, and deemed it harmless, her demeanor would change entirely. She'd stand tall, start sneezing, then prance around, delighted with her own bravery. Thus, a walk was many things—a chance to relieve herself, an adventure out in the larger world away from home, time to meet and play with other dogs, to greet and be petted by strangers and to grow confident that whatever the world or the wind tossed her way, she could handle it.

I'd take her into stores so that I could teach her how to behave in places where it wouldn't be considered polite to sniff or lick things and just three days after she was four months old, I even tried taking her to a restaurant. We went in the late afternoon so that we could just have lemonade and not ask Sky to have to be quiet and unobtrusive for as long as it would take for us to eat a meal. We took Flash along, too, so that he could set the tone for her, which he did. As soon as we sat down, he lay down next to the table and was completely calm. Sky, not knowing what was expected of her, fidgeted. But she kept checking to see what Flash was doing, the way she did at home, and after about five minutes, she lay down next to him and fell asleep. I was pleased to see how quickly she was picking up behaviors that would stand her in good stead for all of her working life.

This was not the first time Sky had observed Flash and then copied his behavior. In fact, she started doing this almost as soon as I brought her home, following him around like a shadow, trying to do whatever he was doing. I had observed dogs learning by watching what older dogs did for most of my life, so I knew that that was one of the ways dogs came to understand the world and the meaning of what human beings were saying to them. Still, what Sky and Flash worked out between them astonished me.

Any job—building a bridge, baking a cake, washing the car, writing a book—can be broken down into steps, as few or as many as required. This is also true of the work a service dog does. There's the overall picture—what the dog is trying to accomplish—helping someone who can't see navigate the world, alerting a deaf person to significant sounds or, in my case, helping with pain. Then there are the steps you take to accomplish that. Dogs that respond to pain need to be with their person all the time because no one can predict when they will be needed. Pain doesn't follow a schedule. So, when I get up to move from one room to another, my service dog gets up and moves with me. Since dogs have an uncanny way of knowing what their people are thinking, my dog often gets to where I am going before I do. Sky watched Flash doing this and the first thing she picked up on was that often, when I got up, I was headed for the bathroom and when I got there, Flash would already be there, waiting for me. In fact, the bathroom was a very appealing place for my dogs. There are always toys in there and once I arrive, there is always a person willing to play. If I were in the bathtub, Flash and I would play with the small, rubber ducks that lined the rim of the tub. I'd toss him a duck. He'd catch it and flip it back into the tub, leaning over the side to watch it splash down, bob up and float. Even sitting on the toilet, I'd play with

Flash, bouncing a ball, tossing a ball, lobbing a ball off the shower door across from where I sat. I felt safer with Flash there and was always ready to make him happy while he stayed close in case he was needed. For his part, Flash knew why he was there and knew there was no harm in having a little fun while he stood in readiness. Sky, on the other hand, hadn't the faintest idea what was going on. She only knew that Flash accompanied me to the bathroom and that once we got there, there was fun to be had. In no time at all, when the bathroom was where I was headed, Sky would get there before me. Pretty soon, she started getting there before Flash. By the time I arrived, she either had the ball, ready to give it to me so that the game could begin, or she'd be standing beside the bathtub, staring at the ducks.

The fact that Sky wanted to join me and Flash in what she might have seen as the game room did not surprise me at all. What did was that no sooner than Sky started running ahead to the bathroom, Flash began to back off. Within a week or so, when I got to the bathroom, Sky would be there and Flash wouldn't. He was old, he was tired, and he was smart enough to recognize help when he saw it. Without any cue from me, Flash began dividing up the work of being a service dog, making sure his assistant was on the job before he let each step go.

As for Sky, she was learning the job from the outside in. Though she had no idea what the purpose of being with me all the time was, she was getting the message to come with me when I moved from one place to another, or to beat me there. Just as in a wolf pack the wolves take responsibility for one another, so it would happen in my little mixed species pack. My job was to let her know when she was on the right track. Even if what she was doing was only step one of a long journey, by praising her, I let her know that she was doing what she should be doing. I'd been through this before. I knew that she would take her own time to learn the job and that she would perform it in her own way.

In the end, she wouldn't be Flash and she wouldn't be Dexter. She would be herself and do things in her own style. That was exactly as it should be. I was fully prepared to accept what she offered me and to understand that her education couldn't and shouldn't be rushed. After all, there were no shortage of reminders that Sky was still a puppy. A few days before acing her first restaurant visit, she tried to shove her nose up mine. A week earlier, she found a way to sit on my head, too. Many mornings, when I woke up and opened my eyes, instead of seeing the sunlight streaming through the blinds, I'd see Sky's hairy belly. When she saw that I was awake, she'd get so happy she'd start sneezing all over me. Then she'd burrow under the covers and wiggle around until she'd managed to toss the blanket onto the floor. Once she "buried" her rawhide bone under the blanket and then tried to dig it out from over the top. Every day she reminded me that, no matter where they live, puppies know how to have fun.

By being with me all the time, Sky would eventually focus on what I was feeling and know whether I felt good or bad. I would be doing the same with her. One day, we would come to know each other as intimately as it was possible to understand a friend who happened to be of another species.

Thanks to Flash and to her working heritage, she had already started to practice the trade that would one day be hers. Meanwhile, though she was only four months old, she was already a writer's dog. As soon as I turned on the computer, she'd stop whatever she was doing and come to be with me, lying near the desk and not interrupting until I was finished working. Good dog, Sky.

4

§ Denise §

Country Dog

The first day we had May all to ourselves, she got pretty much non-stop attention. We threw balls for her to catch, played keep-away with toys and rawhides, cuddled with her and followed her as she ran all over the house exploring. When she'd worn all the rest of us out, we turned her over to one of the adult males, Zeke, also known as the puppy-pooper-outer. True to his reputation, he played with her until she was completely exhausted.

By bedtime, May was still so excited over all the attention, she wasn't ready for it to be over for the day. But over it was, and soon she fell fast asleep all by herself for the first time with no Kate or littermates beside her. May's first day of being the puppy that stayed had been quite a success.

Along with the fun of being a puppy, there was a lot May needed to learn over the next few months. However, it was important for me to plan her new experiences at times when she was ready for them. Just as children learn some things better at certain ages, so do dogs. Children are most successful in learning a foreign language during the time when they're first learning to speak through their preschool years. This is because their brains have the most capacity to take in language skills during the time when they start to communicate with others through speaking. Even though people can learn foreign languages throughout their lives, they pick them up more quickly and easily when their brains are at that perfect early stage.

In dogs, there are known ages when their brains are most prepared to take in certain information and experiences. From the time a puppy usually leaves to go to its new home at around seven to eight weeks, until about three months, its brain is like a sponge, ready to soak up new social situations and experiences. This is a critical time to help a puppy adjust to the world it will live in. If it doesn't have that experience at the right time, sometimes the dog can never quite catch up socially As they age, dogs seem to lose flexibility to adjust to new social situations.

As well as paying close attention to the mental stages when May would learn certain things best, I needed to know when her body was physically able to handle certain activities. She wouldn't be ready for formal training on sheep until she was about a year old. Moving and controlling sheep takes a strong body, a mature mind, and the ability, both physically and mentally, to stick with the job until it's done. Her training to be a sheepdog would involve using all of her natural instincts and also the self-control to ignore those same instincts when the work called for it. As a growing pup, she would hopefully be excited by seeing sheep, and would perhaps show me some quick glimpses of promise of the working dog she could become, but she wouldn't be able to handle the pressure of all the specific tasks involved in learning to be a useful sheepdog.

While Sky's job for the first few months after leaving the farm was becoming accustomed to the sights and sounds of a lively and noisy big city, May would only need to learn to deal with the lesser challenges of living on a small farm. For the next few months, May's job was to become a "good dog"—to come when called, pay attention to her human partner, and to respect the hierarchy among the dogs on the farm and dogs she would meet when I took her on adventures away from home. Some of what May would have to learn would be the same as what any dog needs to know, like chewing her toys and not the furniture, and eliminating out-of-doors and not on the Oriental rug. Other things—like learning to obey certain commands reliably, such as coming when called no matter what she's doing or how far away she is, and the development of self-control in general—would help set the groundwork for her attitude toward a variety of situations she might face as an adult. This training would also help May cement her relationship with me even before we start doing sheep work.

As well as learning a few specific word commands, May would need to learn to interpret the information-rich interaction of body language and voice tones for communication between us in everyday life. She would learn about me and I would learn about her mostly through being together. No commands would be needed for ninety percent of what she would learn to understand simply from living with us day to day as she grew up. She would figure out her position in our little pack and how she fit into the overall structure of our lives. Even though she would need to learn the boundaries, and probably re-learn some of them, she would gather information as she matured that would allow her to generalize ways that she was expected to behave. Border collies tend to be very perceptive dogs at understanding what types or classes of behaviors are allowed and not allowed simply by understanding the rules of one or more behaviors. When she learned a certain rude behavior was not allowed, she would come to understand other similarly rude behaviors were also undesirable. So starting the very next morning after the other puppies left, it was time to begin May's journey to becoming a "good dog."

For the first few days, May, now the youngest among the human and dog family members, suddenly seemed less independent and feisty than she had been when her littermates were here. For a time, she had been leader of the pack of puppies. Now, hanging out with the grown up dogs, she was low man on the totem pole.

But May quickly adjusted to her new status and began to fit in with our family life fairly easily. That's not to say she wasn't still a bit full of herself. The process of having a puppy seamlessly grow into the perfect adult never goes quite as planned. And that's not such a bad thing, since it would deprive the family of enjoying each dog's journey of struggles and triumphs.

As a little puppy, it was hard not to overlook a little of May's bratty playfulness here and there, however, and even enjoy it. She loved to steal toys and rawhide chewies from the older dogs. She would fawn and beg and do a great imitation of a sad, pitiful puppy when she wanted a rawhide or toy from the others. She must've still had her "puppy

license," because they usually let her have them after a fake show of defending the prize.

But even indulgent dogs have their limits. Sometimes, instead of acting cute, May would bark right in their faces to get attention. On those occasions, the older dogs would sometimes gently discipline her by nipping at her to get her to stop. Even that didn't always work. After a few minutes, she'd be back, bouncing around and barking in their faces all over again. The other dogs were generally a lot more tolerant of her bratty puppy ways than I would have expected. I was curious to see how long this tolerance would last.

Like many pups, May figured out ways to entertain people so they would keep paying attention to her. My daughter had a huge stuffed green turtle her boyfriend won for her at the fair. May invented a game where she bounced on the side of the turtle, went up in the air, landed on her head, and tumbled over on the very top of the turtle's soft shell. She used the turtle like a trampoline. At first I thought she was doing it by accident until she started working on standing on her head on it without the acrobatics. It was a very calculated effort, like a kid carefully trying to do a headstand or tumble. What a nut!

May's mom, Kate, like her own mom, Molly, loved to jump up on things—anything two to three feet high was fair game. In fact, they would naturally jump up on and run across the backs of sheep when in packed areas, something not all sheepdogs can even be taught to do. But a love of heights was in their blood, and it was passed down through the generations quite dominantly. In the house, they would almost levitate onto the furniture. They were on the floor then—poof—there they were on the couch before you could even blink. It was such a strong tendency in them, we decided early on to allow them on the furniture, which was leather and easy to clean. This was fortunate because May was not only a levitator like Molly and Kate, she was a levitator extraordinaire. She could jump on the couch, grab a pillow, throw it high in the air, jump down, catch it before it landed and be up on the chair across the room before you could say "May." We knew to be careful about letting young puppies with developing bones jump down off of heights; thankfully, the couches and chairs weren't very high, and we watched her carefully to keep her from getting too wild. Still, we all enjoyed her occasional antics and frequent puppy "zoomies," where she tore about the house like a

mad thing, zigging and zagging and sprinting in between. She was developing the coordination and speed she would need as an adult, but it looked like all fun to us. It was the dead of winter and we spent a lot of time in the den with a nice fire in the fireplace, playing with and watching the dogs play. It was a fun time. A new puppy always brings a special joy and life into our

family and May was no exception.

May also had more than her share of sweet ways with both us and the other dogs. She was very affectionate with the older dogs, especially Molly, her grandmother. Molly was 14 years old at the time, and May would cuddle and curl all against her. Like wolf cubs begging for food or showing deference to their elders, May would also lick

Molly's muzzle and sometimes even stick her whole snout into Molly's mouth. Molly tolerated and apparently enjoyed this seemingly annoying behavior. Go figure! Because muzzle licking is a normal social ritual among dogs and wolves, I've rarely seen an adult dog get cranky over this behavior. One thing she did with me that was quite endearing was to press her nose and mouth against the side of my cheek and just hold it there. No licks, just cold puppy nose and lips mashed against my face for several seconds. It felt good. I've never had a dog do that specifically, although all of my dogs like to "kiss" me with licks on the face.

Even though May had plenty of time just to be a puppy, she needed to learn some self-control. Early on, I began crate training for her, where she would spend a little bit of time each day in a small plastic crate. I extended the time she was in the crate until she was sleeping in it all night and spending an hour or two napping in it a couple of times during the day. Wolves live in dens where they normally spend many hours a day. It's only natural that dogs would take well to den-like areas such as dog crates.

I find crate training important for a number of reasons. I use a crate that's big enough for the puppy to lie down comfortably, but not a whole lot bigger than that. Puppies have a natural desire to keep their sleeping area clean, so they learn pretty quickly not to pee and poop until they are let out. This helps quite a bit in housetraining a pup. Of course, it only works if the puppy is allowed to get used to the crate slowly, and if it's not kept in the crate for more than an hour or two at a time during the day to start with. There are many people opposed to "locking dogs up" in crates, thinking it cruel for the dog. In reality, most dogs come to love their crate's den-like atmosphere. It's quite natural for them to sleep and "hang out" in crates. It helps them to feel safe in what is, for them, a sometimes hectic world.

In addition, spending quiet time in crates helps pups learn to settle and develop an "off switch." Working Border collies are bred to be active dogs. Some of them can become what people consider "hyper." Although a lot of interaction and activity can help use up excess energy, it's important to raise them with the expectation that they learn to control themselves as they grow up and are able to do so. In my experience, there can be a fairly wide natural range of activity levels in pups, even within the same litter. They're not all capable of being couch potatoes no matter how you raise them. While it's unreasonable to expect them all to be the same, or be capable of being trained all to be the same activity level, it's fair to expect a pup to learn restraint within the boundaries of its natural tendencies.

After the normal amount of fussing to be let out, May quickly came to love her crate and sometimes even went in there on her own when she was tired. After she became used to it, she was happy to stay in it for up to two hours at a time during the day and all night as long as she wasn't hungry or needing to use the bathroom. When she would start "squeaking," it usually meant she needed something. She rarely took advantage and only asked to be let out when she had a good reason. May was probably the easiest pup to crate train that I've ever had.

As always, along with the good comes some bad. As she got older, May's barking became more pronounced. She continued to bark in the other dogs' faces to get attention or while playing. Not only did May bark while playing, she started barking when up at the barn in her kennel, where she stayed part of the day when the weather was nice. Then she started barking when excited while running around in the yard. Not having had a bad barker before, I didn't realize this bad habit was forming in time to catch it before it got out of hand. Now, it will always be a problem I'll have to work to control.

As she grew up, May began to show some breed-specific traits. She had seen and paid a little passing attention to

sheep on the other side of the fence from the time she was first in the yard at a few weeks old. When she was about ten weeks old, she suddenly took more notice of the sheep. I was relieved and excited to see this, because sometimes even a well-bred pup from parents who are both working border collies will never show any interest in sheep at all. However, as glad as I was, as soon as I noticed she was showing a keener interest in the sheep, I was careful not to allow her to spend time staring at them or trying to work them from the other side of the fence. This type of thing is one of the most common ways a border collie puppy can be ruined before it ever even starts its training on sheep. Working a border collie on sheep is a three-way relationship between the dog, the trainer, and the sheep. Dogs need to associate their experiences with sheep, especially the early ones, with their trainer as well.

When May was around three months old, I took her and my other dogs on several trips out of town to work the adult dogs on the sheep at friends' farms. While there, May got to play with some of her littermates—Moss, Sweep, and Leia.

They picked up as if they had never been apart and had a grand old time tussling about and play fighting.

The last visit's play session was high-lighted by May accidentally jump-ing into a small pond by following Moss in during a game of chase. Although she was able to swim immediately, the look on her face when she hit the water was priceless. She immediately made a U-turn and swam to shore, but in her usual bold manner was right back in the water within minutes.

On that same trip I tried the three littermates there, Moss, Leia, and May, one at a time, on a small group of quiet sheep just to see if they were "turned on" to working sheep with a person yet. Using an experienced dog to help, all three pups showed good promise for their age. Because they were just young puppies, I only tried them each for a few minutes, and didn't do any kind of training with them. We kept the situation in control so they could easily handle it and have a good experience. As I did with all my pups, I would continue to do this with May once a month or so to briefly check her interest until she was closer to a year old.

When I go to sheepdog trials, I usually take most of the dogs with me, so it's important that they like to travel. May seemed to enjoy these first outings, playing happily with the other puppies in an area out of sight of where the adult dogs were working sheep. As an extra treat, I let May snuggle with me on the bed in my small motor home some of the nights while we were visiting. Even though she hadn't been many places off the farm, she seemed comfortable both with the long trips and with spending time away from home in a strange place. She did get a little car sick on the way, but overall, she traveled well, and seemed to feel quite at home at each new place we went.

One of the most important parts of May becoming a "good dog" those first few months was to learn to come when called. For pet dogs and many other working dogs, the command is "come." For sheepdogs, it's "that'll do." No matter what the command is, all pups need to learn to come when called. Since our farm is completely fenced, I was able to take my time teaching May to come. My goal was to develop a bomb-proof recall in her by the time she was ready to start real training on sheep. Developing her recall was to be the first formal step in the development of our partnership on sheep.

Like most very young pups, May naturally came to people for attention early on. As soon as she was able to do this, I started to use the body language and words or sounds that she could naturally associate with this behavior. When she was very young—less than eight weeks—I started calling her in a high cheerful voice saying, "pup, pup" to get her attention. Most pups will come to such sounds. I would often squat down or sit on the ground in order to seem less threatening by being more on her level. When adult dogs lie down, it signals a pup that it's okay to glom all over them. My sitting on the ground gave May the same message. It was a natural signal for her to come for affection. Using these things helped her to understand to come to me in the beginning.

As pups get older and more independent, they tend to test the limits, just as human kids do. When this happened with May at around four months of age, I didn't even try to call her to me unless we were in a small, enclosed space, like in the barn or the house. Then, if she ran away instead of coming, I simply followed her until she got as far as the enclosure allowed her to go. I then called her again, sometimes using more engaging body language such as kneeling down or patting my thigh or maybe getting very close to her. Eventually, she figured out there was nowhere else to go and coming to me was a better idea. Once she did this, she got "loved on" for a bit for making a good choice. I repeated this procedure over and over in larger and larger enclosed areas as she grew and became more reliable at coming. It took several months of careful planning and training in the right situations to convince May that coming when called was a requirement, not an option. She certainly had her share of disobedience from time to time, but because she was never allowed to run away and not come from the very beginning, she eventually stopped even thinking about not coming.

Living on the farm gave me an advantage when teaching May to come out in the wide-open spaces. When we walked in the field for daily exercise, the other dogs already knew to come when called. The entire field was fenced, so the dogs were allowed to wander and explore at will on these walks. When the dogs were some distance from me, I used a whistle for "that'll do" rather than a voice command. The whistle carries much farther than the human voice, so shepherds all over the world use it when working with sheepdogs. When they heard the "that'll do" whistle, all my adult dogs would stop what they were doing and come running. May naturally followed the others back to me when I called them. I made a point of calling all the dogs back to me several times on each of these walks to help May learn to come by copying the older dogs. The other dogs always came back to me at a dead run. Soon May was doing that, too. She wanted to be part of the "race" and would come running as fast as her little puppy legs could take her. Now I had two ways to call May. By doing what the pack did, she'd learned to respond to both a voice and a whistle command. She'd come right away, even from very far away.

When I communicated with May using my voice, I tried to make my voice a tone she wanted to hear. As a very young puppy, I used a high, exciting voice. As she matured and our relationship and communication grew, I used more variation in tone and emotion to convey my feelings to her. When she was good, I tried in as genuine a way as possible to make my voice like silk, a sound she would love to hear, a sound she would seek and listen for. If she didn't hear the voice she loved, I wanted her to care and try to figure out what it took to hear it again. I could use her name expressively to convey almost any message, depending on how I said it. "May" could mean "bad dog" or "you silly thing" or "I love you" or "I'm so frustrated with you right now" or any number of things. This conveying of my feelings simply through tone and emotion and her understanding of it would need to expand and become highly refined as she was trained on sheep. Along with the sheep's reactions to her, it would be part of the subtle feedback system that would quickly shape the development of her inborn talent.

When she was four months old, May went to the vet for her first rabies shot. I had given her the first puppy vaccines at home so she had never been to the vet. Besides our trips to the farms and houses of friends, and the odd trip to the feed store and the like, May had not been in public around other dogs and people very much. Nevertheless, she marched into the vet's office door pulling ahead on her leash, positive she had found a new place with friends who would pet and adore her. Her expectations were promptly met, as everyone ogled all over her from the second she walked in the door. The staff at the vet's office always tried to make the visits a good experience, especially for puppies. They made a huge fuss over her and, of course, May ate it up, practicing her soft brown sweet puppy-face look until she was sure that every last person there had melted. She barely noticed when the shot was given to her, and when we left she still thought it a great place to visit. Our first vet trip had been a good experience all the way around.

By its nature, farm life involves the seasonal variation in work for both me and the dogs. If the weather is good, summer is usually the easiest time of the year, with the main dog work being to help sort and wean lambs, vaccinate lambs, worm the whole flock, and perhaps move them from pasture to pasture. In the fall, sheep must be sorted, the ram is put in for breeding, and daily feeding starts as the summer grass dies back. By winter, there's no grass to eat, so the ewes must be fed a couple of times a day. Most of the winter work revolves around getting the sheep to feed no matter what the weather is like. With spring, of course, comes lambing and all the work that goes with that.

That spring, May turned four months old as my lambing season began. There are normally a few weeks during lambing season when my time is concentrated on the sheep night and day, and this year things were even more hectic. I had five of what are called bottle lambs. These are lambs that, for whatever reason, their mothers aren't able to or won't feed. Aside from checking the ewes day and night to make sure they weren't having problems having their babies, and helping the new mothers and their lambs, Erin or I had to feed hungry orphan lambs several times a day for about a month until they could eat solid food.

Even though I was busy, I tried working May on the sheep a time or two during her fourth month, just to make sure she was still interested. She was. In additional preparation for her career as a sheepdog, she got to hear the normal constant noise of ewes and lambs calling out to each other, with the special bonus of especially loud screaming lambs when it was time for their bottle. Lambing time is just another part of farm life, and May found it all very exciting and interesting.

Although Erin and Jim, and of course the other dogs, had plenty of time for May, that month she didn't get the attention from me that she was used to. When I would come in tired from the barn after my lambing and sheep chores were over for the day and flop down on the couch, a still-pretty little puppy named May would levitate up beside me, gently pressing her mouth against my cheek and just holding it there. How could anybody feel bad after that?

By the end of May's fourth month, she had ridden in vehicles of various sorts, taken a few trips to different farms, spent several nights in a motor home, swum in a pond, become interested in sheep and worked them a little bit with me as her leader, seen and heard a bunch of newborn lambs, learned to come when called, been out about all over the farm quite a bit, learned to accept that it was quiet time when put in a crate, had her first vet visit, and become reliably house trained. Mostly, though, she had played and played.

5

§ Carol §

Growing Up Canine: Sky's Story

One day, when Flash was about three and a half years old, I was working on a book and suddenly was overwhelmed by pain. The pain from Crohn's disease can come on suddenly, like an ocean wave when a big ship passes. One minute you're fine, the next you're drowning in it.

The couch seemed too far away, so I did what I often did when this happened. I got off the chair and lay down on the rug. There was something comforting about being on the floor when I was hurting. For one thing, I couldn't fall.

Flash had learned not to bother me when I was working and he was very good about that. But the moment my fingers were off the keyboard, his fervent belief was that now my job was to play with him. Lying on the floor, I heard his nails clicking in the short hallway between my office and the living room and then sound and silence would alternate as he ran across the rug and then back onto the wooden floor looking for just the right toy to bring me to throw for him. Suddenly the sound of his nails on the floor stopped altogether. For what seemed like a long time, the house was quiet. When I heard him again, he was doing something he never, ever did. He was walking. Even going across a room, Flash would lope. He would always try to go as quickly as possible, even when he was on leash. But this time, he walked back to where I was and now I could see that history was about to be made again. He came back without a toy.

He stood over me, clearly perplexed. I looked up at him. His eyes were searching my face, looking for a clue. His forehead was pleated with worry. His tail was down and he was very still. He knew something was wrong and somehow he knew that it was his job to fix it. Unfortunately, just then, he had no idea how. Nonetheless, right before my eyes, Flash had grown up.

I praised him like crazy. It was Flash's "aha" moment and I wanted to let him know that he was on the right track. Looking back, had I stayed silent, I don't think it would have mattered. Flash didn't need my approval. He had seen his life's work.

It took very little time for Flash to get the answer he was looking for and because it's always nice to receive recognition, even if you're a dog, I continued to praise him for each step in the right direction. Soon enough, when I felt bad, Flash would be right there with me. He'd lie against me, and in what would seem like no time at all, the pain would diminish. Sometimes I'd be able to get up and go about my business. Other times, particularly on those occasions where I'd made it to the bed, I'd fall asleep. When I'd wake up, no matter if it was night and I'd slept through to the morning, Flash would be there, pressed up against me, doing his job.

For Sky, things happened in an entirely different way. Sky was learning how to be a service dog by copying what Flash did. She hadn't had a blinding moment of insight, the way he had. On the other hand, he was nearly four when that happened. Sky began working when she was still just a pup.

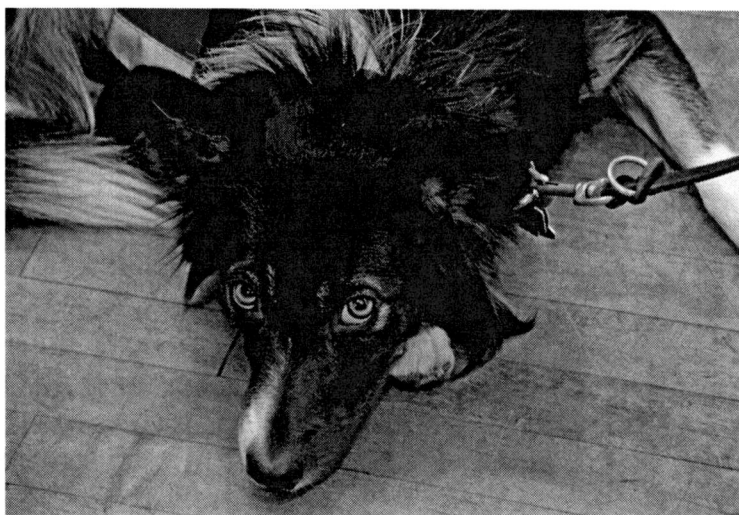

While humans may fail to communicate with their dogs from time to time, and while dogs may fail to make it clear to us what it is they need at a given moment, these glitches rarely happen dog to dog. Flash spoiled Sky, just as we did, playing with her whenever she wanted to play, letting her take toys from his mouth and even food from his dish, but as the older and more experienced of the two, it was always clear that he was the top dog. Like the mother dog who lets her puppies pull on her ears and tail, growling and acting like little toughs, when the game is over, Flash made it clear that it was just a game, not real life. He never had to do anything special to get this message across. It's just the way it was and they both knew it.

Even though she almost always got her way, stealing the chew toy or running off with the ball, Sky looked up to Flash. She followed him when he was up and about, lay down next to him when he needed rest, and above all, wanted nothing more than to be just like him and to do whatever he did. Sky was learning how to act like a service dog early on, long before she could understand *why* she was doing what she was doing.

I praised Sky when she showed up in the bathroom ready to play or moved with me from room to room, looking up at my face the way Flash did, but it was Flash who did most of the teaching at home. Still, there was work for me, too. There was a whole world outside our home for Sky to experience in order for her to become comfortable in all the places she'd go as a working service dog. There were good manners she had to learn, behaviors far and above what pet dogs need. And there was the enrichment she needed in order not to be thrown by changes. So we continued to explore, sometimes with Flash and sometimes without him. Going out with Flash meant that Sky would always be able to look to him to help her figure out if something was okay or not. Going out without him meant she was thrown on her own resources, that she herself would have to figure out how to feel comfortable and safe in new situations. Both kinds of experiences were important. If I always took Flash, Sky would continue to depend on him. That wasn't good, because eventually she'd have to be out there on her own, not only trying new things, but watching me at the same time to see if I needed her help.

There was one part of her job Sky saw on her own without any assistance from Flash or from me. I found this out early on, when she was still very young, and it was interesting because it was a natural extension of what Denise saw shortly after the puppies were born. Sky was tuned into emotions. She was barely three months old the first time something made me cry since I'd brought her home. She was playing with a toy, tossing it in the air and pouncing on it, growling fiercely when she picked it up again. She was completely occupied, or so I thought. And then my tears came and Sky dropped the toy and came running. I was sitting on the edge of the bed and she came up, placed her paws on my shoulders and licked away my tears. In no time, I felt better and immediately went to the computer to write Denise.

A couple of months later, I found out that my pup's empathetic behavior was not restricted to me. Sky had gotten comfortable in restaurants and a few places we liked had enough room between tables for two dogs. We always tried our best to go when the restaurants were not jammed with other people, but once, on a really pretty, sunny day, apparently everyone in the neighborhood had the same idea we did. There were people on both sides of us and just enough room for everyone to fit if we didn't fidget around too much. We were happily eating lunch when the baby at the next table began to cry, the kind of wail only a baby can produce. Her face became all red and scrunched up. All the cuddling and bouncing her parents tried did nothing to allay her misery. Sky was watching carefully, her forehead wrinkled in worry. She adored children of all ages and was especially tender with babies. Finally, she got up and gently placed her paws on the father's thigh, which made her barely tall enough for the baby to notice her. Instantly, the crying stopped. The baby's eyes became round and large, her mouth opened slightly into a smile. Had I not been absolutely sure Sky was safe with babies, I would have called her back. But I was sure. The father tilted the baby downward and Sky licked the tears from her little apple cheeks, then came back to me all on her own.

As a city dog, Sky needed to learn the basic commands. The streets were crowded with people and other dogs, baby strollers and shopping carts and people talking on their cell phones and texting rather than looking where they were going. There were times when Sky was able to walk out front at the end of the leash or sniff sniff sniff along the curb, but at other times, it was safer for her to be at my side. The word that told her to do that was "heel," my absolute worst command with border collies. I walk pretty fast, but not as fast as a border collie. Sky had the stamina of her mother, Kate, and the stocky muscles of her father,

Scott. She was so small and quick, she barely seemed to touch the ground when she ran. But when you hugged her or picked her up, she felt like a little linebacker. Like Flash at her age, she never seemed to get tired. At the end of a two- or three-mile walk, she'd barely be warmed up. Of course, I threw the ball for her before I'd head out—and that helped a little. But heel was definitely a challenge for us.

The other commands, sit, down, stay, and come were pieces of cake. I started each one at home, with Flash as my assistant. I'd say, "sit." Flash would sit. Sky would look at Flash. Sky would sit. Done deal.

She learned everything this way. She understood that when she didn't know what a word meant, Flash did. Like every dog I've ever had who came to live in a home with an older dog, she knew just where to look to find out the meaning of what I was saying. It was the most natural thing in the world for her to learn by observing an older member of her pack.

What was interesting is that while I sometimes struggled over getting her to walk at my pace, if I took her someplace where pet dogs couldn't normally go, a restaurant or the market and eventually, the gym where I went swimming, she would behave perfectly. It seemed like a judgment call. It was as if she could see the reason for containing herself in some settings, but saw no reason for it in others. It was hard to argue with her logic. I'd seen it before, particularly with Dexter, my first service dog. He was content to be on the leash in the city, but take him to the country or even to a park, and the leash made no sense to him. If there was an acre or more of grass, Dexter thought he should be off leash and able to run. That was dog logic and it always seemed pretty sound to me.

City dogs also learn commands like "leave it," which means "please refrain from scarfing up pizza and chicken bones from the sidewalk." After learning that meaning, "leave it" magically expands to mean, "ignore whatever you're looking at—it's none of your business." At that point, the command can be used (and has been used) to deter a pup from heading toward an iffy looking dog at the dog park, or eyeing the steak her partner is about to eat.

Sky learned "take it," which was the command for retrieving, in a nano second. She didn't need a command. Toss a ball and she'd go get it, once, twice, or fifty times. But putting it on cue meant I could work on all her other commands while I played ball with her. The motivation was built in—the chance to retrieve.

It meant more to her than that pizza she had to pass on the sidewalk or the steak I'd ask her to forget about.

Once Sky knew what the commands meant, I would take her to the park in front of my building and tell her to "wait," to "stay," or to "lie down," whatever commands I wanted to practice that day. Then I'd toss the ball and tell her "take it." I'd discovered with Flash that the tighter you screw things down, the happier a border collie is. If you make it tough, precise and challenging, they simply could not be happier. So most of Sky's training, especially the off-leash work, happened during a game of fetch where I could challenge her mind as she worked her body.

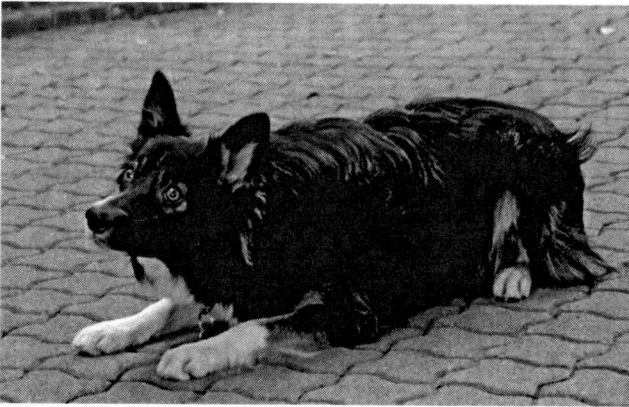

Service dogs need their own set of commands, words appropriate for whatever work they are going to do. Guide dogs learn the command "forward." Some mobility dogs, dogs who help people in wheelchairs, learn to put on and shut off the lights on command, and some even will bring a soda from the refrigerator if asked.

When I was little and needed to rest, my grandmother, Fanny, would sit next to me, pat her lap and tell me, "Lay keppie," meaning *put your sweet little head here*. When Flash was younger and first came to help me, he'd lay his sweet head against the place that hurt, looking up at me with his soft, brown eyes to see if I was feeling better yet. So, naturally, "keppie" became the word for pressing against me when I was in pain. Unlike "sit" and "down" and "come," I rarely used "keppie" as a command. Instead, I used it as praise, telling Flash "Good keppie," when he came to help me on his own.

Once in a blue moon, when I thought there were too many distractions for my dog to notice I was hurting, I'd use "keppie" as a request or, perhaps, a reminder. Once, for example, Flash and I were walking on a busy street when a wave of pain found me. Up ahead, at the side of a movie theater, there was a short flight of steps leading to a door, the fire door, perhaps. I sat on the steps and whispered "keppie" because with all the distractions in the street, I didn't know if he would have done it on his own. In fact, he probably would have. I was the one who tended to ignore my pain, not Flash.

One time, he'd gotten up on his hind legs in the movies and pressed himself against me. I got very upset, thinking everyone in the movie house would think I had an untrained dog who wouldn't lie down quietly during the film. I stupidly corrected him, telling him to lie down, not once but at least three times. Then I took my attention off the movie and put it on what was happening. He was my partner, worthy of my trust. He tried again and that time I let him, immediately feeling the pain start to abate. I'd gotten very good at living in my own little world and making believe I wasn't in pain when I was. But Flash wasn't fooled and would not stop trying until I let him do his job. This is one of the reasons why I chose to work with border collies. Any dog that's bred to convince a ram to go left when it wants to go right has enough toughness to convince a stubborn human she needs help even when she herself doesn't know it. Flash was always up for the job. I was the one who needed frequent reminders of the way things were:

Pain knows where I am.

Dog knows where pain is.

Dog conquers pain.

I followed the same pattern with Sky. Instead of teaching her to lean against me on command, I let her figure that out herself and praised her when she did. Help feels better when it is offered voluntarily. So when Sky came into bed and threw herself against my side, because she'd seen Flash do that, or because she was happy to be there for pats and kisses because it made *her* feel good, I whispered "good keppie" in her ear, keeping up the family tradition. By giving the help she gave me a name, I am able to let her know that when she presses tight against me, it makes me feel as safe and happy as when I used to lay my head in my grandmother's lap. When Sky is older, on those rare occasions when she might not know I need her help, I can politely request it.

Every dog's life needs balance, time to work, time to play and time off to rest. Sky had all this. She was learning her job, she was playing ball, and she had Flash with whom she could and did play morning, noon and night. But even though she played with lots of other dogs, she apparently also needed something else, a best friend close to her own age with whom she could share a special bond. When she was about eight months old, our very good friends Richard and Polly came for dinner with their new puppy, an eight-week-old German shorthair pointer they'd named Nellie. It was love at first bite. We sat out in our yard while the girls chewed on each other, raced in circles, tugged at toys and became forever friends. Whenever we got together, at our house, at their house, or upstate at their country house, the two pups would play as if they'd been together all the time, with no break at all. They seemed to speak the same language, a precious thing. As with human beings, that's not true with everyone you meet.

Around the time that Sky and Nellie met and became fast friends, my husband, Steve, got very sick and was in the hospital. Sky had been going to restaurants and riding on the bus, but she hadn't done any of the really difficult work a service dog is called upon to do. Now I had a dilemma. Flash had reached the point where he couldn't go into a hospital. The floors are usually light colored and very shiny and some dogs, when they get old, can no longer navigate floors that are slippery and reflect light. Sometimes, after they slip once, they become afraid of slick floors. Plus, and this is just a guess, the reflected light might make it difficult for them to see well. There was no way I could take him with me to visit Steve. Nor was there any way I could do something so stressful without a service dog. So I drafted Sky, slipped her cape on her, and headed for St. Vincent's Hospital, just a few blocks from home.

St. Vincent's is huge, divided into different buildings, with long halls connecting one to another. After we got a visitor's pass, we started down one long hall toward the elevators that would take us up to the wing where Steve's room was. The floor was slick and I wondered if I'd have to pick Sky up, but she walked as if she were here every day of her life. In fact, she led the way, acting as if she knew exactly where she was going. Her walk was determined, head up, tail down. Collies lower their tails when they are working. At seven months old, because she was needed, Sky had stepped up into the job. When we got to the appropriate bank of elevators, we waited in a sea of doctors, the little dark tri among all those white coats, sitting as calmly as if she belonged exactly where she was. In fact, she did.

As soon as we got into Steve's room, Sky hopped onto his bed and began to kiss him. He didn't look too bad and seemed happy to see us. I pulled up a chair and we talked for a bit. The curtain between the beds was closed and we didn't see Steve's roommate, but when he began to cough, Sky jumped off Steve's bed to try to go and comfort him. Since he was keeping to himself, I didn't think that would be a good idea, but was very touched that that was what she wanted to do.

When Sky first came to live with us, she had coppery brown markings on her cheeks, amazingly, in the shape of hearts.

Unlike the spots on Dalmatians, the brown markings on tri color collies change. As Sky matured, the hearts morphed into flecks of copper that glowed in the sunshine. But Sky hadn't changed on the inside. Even without hearts on her cheeks, she was as empathetic as ever. At home, she'd even go up to the TV when someone sounded distressed, standing right by one of the speakers, her head cocked in attention. I thought, given the chance, she'd like to cheer up every patient in the hospital.

On our way out of the hospital, we passed a model of a human head with all the veins showing. I could barely stand to look at it, but Sky thought it was the greatest thing since bone-shaped dog biscuits. She pulled me over to the counter where it stood, put her paws up near it and craned her neck forward. She sniffed the head for a long time. I kept my eyes averted so that I wouldn't see it. There's no accounting for tastes. The incident reminded me, as I am often reminded, that though I have loved and studied dogs all my life, I will never understand them completely. Though I think of myself as part dog, I am, alas, merely human.

At home, Sky and Flash and I felt very sad. We moped around, missing Steve. Most days, I'd come home, take Flash for a walk, then go back to the hospital again. On my second visit on Friday, something terrific happened. I followed Sky into Steve's room and instead of smiling, he frowned. He began immediately to complain about the food. Then he told me all the other things he didn't like about the hospital. "I want a turkey sandwich," he told me. "And the newspaper. Bring a pen so that I can do the puzzle." He was really grouchy and may have wondered why I stood there grinning. Getting annoyed in the hospital is usually a good sign someone's getting better. The next morning I took both dogs and went to the farmers' market three blocks from our house. I bought some smoked turkey for Steve's sandwich, baby lettuce, cucumbers to make the sandwich crisp, and fresh bread. When I got home, I made the sandwich. I put some cookies in the bag. And the newspaper. I even remembered the pen.

Sky and I left early to bring Steve his sandwich. I couldn't wait to see him. I was sure he'd have better color and that he'd continue to be grouchy, wanting to go home. But as soon as Sky and I got off on his floor, we knew something was wrong. Even before we turned the last corner to the corridor to his room, it was too noisy. Once we turned that corner, there were too many people and too many machines and they were all outside Steve's room. When we pushed our way in, four people were bent over the bed and they were moving Steve to a gurney. One of the doctors came over to me. "We're taking him to the ICU," she said. "You can come in about ten minutes, but first pack up all his things." They started down the hall and then stopped. Someone picked up Steve's left hand and pulled off his wedding band, coming back to where I was standing and handing it to me. "You better hang onto this," she said, and a moment later they had pushed the gurney around the corner and were gone. No one had told me what was wrong.

I'm sure my mouth was hanging open and that Sky was whining, but I can't swear to any of that. I was too stunned. We'd been shoved out into the hall so that the gurney could make the turn and stood there now in the empty hall. I had no idea what was going on and, apparently, neither did Steve because when the gurney had passed where I was standing, he hadn't looked in my direction.

A nurse gave me some paper shopping bags and I packed up Steve's things. I was surprised at how much was there after just a few days in the hospital. After we did that, I asked where the ICU was and still holding onto the bag with the turkey sandwich and the newspaper, Sky and I headed for the elevators.

As soon as I got to the ICU, I knew it was no place for a puppy. Even the air tasted different. Everyone waiting in the large waiting area was tense to the moon and if you weren't terrified before you got there, you were terrified a moment later. I was told they were doing a "procedure" on Steve and that we couldn't come and see him. I was told it would take an hour or two.

For a long time, Sky and I sat and waited. I kept giving her water and finally realized that she was so thirsty because she was stressed. I thought maybe food would distract her and there was no way Steve was going to eat his turkey sandwich so I took it out of the bag and sitting in the ICU waiting room, I pulled out most of the turkey for Sky. I took a bite myself but had no appetite at all. I just wanted water, drinking out of the same cup as Sky.

After an hour or so, one of the doctor's came out. She said that while service dogs were allowed in most of the hospital, they couldn't let Sky into the ICU because they did sterile procedures there. I told her I'd already decided it was no place for a dog. I told her I'd take her home and come right back. Sky would have stayed in the waiting room with me all day. She already knew, at seven months of age, that her job was to take care of me. But mine was to take care of her, and there was too much tension in the air outside the ICU. It was no place for a puppy, even if that puppy was a service dog. When she was very little, Sky had learned to kiss on the lips, almost like a person. We usually did that before heading out from home. I bent toward her and she lifted her muzzle and put her mouth up against mine. Then we walked down a short hallway to the elevator that would take us downstairs. The noisy city seemed very quiet as we walked home, as if it were sad, too.

Flash was excited to see us, but as he did every time I returned from the hospital, he looked behind me to see if Steve was there. I took him out for a short walk, kissed both dogs and went back to the hospital alone.

Steve was the only patient in the ICU who was awake and talking—everyone else seemed to be in sorry shape—so all the nurses hung out in his room. He had a lot of attention and wonderful care. In a few days, he was in a regular room again, complaining like crazy. Sky started visiting again which was an enormous help to me. A few days later, Steve came home.

At seven months of age, Sky had made an incredible leap. Sometimes, circumstances require dogs—or people—

to make sudden changes. Because she was well bred, of working parents, had been well socialized and had Flash as a mentor, Sky had been able to take a giant step into her life's work. Meanwhile, once Steve was home, Flash started taking care of him. Quietly, with no fuss at all, he'd get up onto the end of the bed and spend the day there, watching Steve. At night, after his last walk, he'd lie down next to me, pressing himself as close to my body as possible so that, despite all the work and worry, I could sleep.

For a while, I was too busy taking care of Steve and the dogs to do anything else. By September, though, I was able to go swimming again. Once more, I had a difficult decision to make. Flash was two months short of twelve by then. It was a long walk to the gym and soon enough, the weather would be getting cold. Shortly after that, there'd be snow. I wanted to keep Flash working but I was starting to think it might not be fair to him. He was conflicted, too. Sometimes, when he felt tired, he'd go off by himself, hoping, it seemed, that everyone would leave him alone. Yet if I put Sky's cape on her, there he'd be, at the door, looking heartbroken. No matter how old they are, dogs that were bred to work don't ever want to quit. Work was the heart of Flash's life.

When I begin working with a new pup, whenever possible I stick to the easy things. I let the dog wear a service dog cape on some walks, just to get used to it. Next I begin taking the dog to restaurants, with the older, more experienced dog along as a mentor. I save the hard work, doctor visits, the gym, business trips, for the seasoned service dog, the one who won't get flustered by strange sights and sounds or long waits in the airport. Now, I switched the dogs' roles. It was Sky who began to do the more difficult work and Flash who got to lie next to the table and sample my dinner when Steve and I went out to eat. Flash would go along when Steve got a haircut or needed to go to the bank. Sky, who had proved herself worthy of her tag and little red cape when Steve was in the hospital, came with me to the gym when I was able to take the time again.

The gym is a difficult place for a young dog because there's a lot of distraction, a lot of strange looking machines, a lot of humans grunting with effort, a lot of waiting and, most challenging, part of the time there's nothing to hook the leash to and the dog is loose. By the third visit, Sky was comfortable enough with the routine to lead the way. She'd take me to the desk to check in, stop where I picked up a robe, make the turn into the ladies locker room so that I could change and lead the way up the stairs and over a sort of bridge to get to the pool. At the pool, I was able to hook her leash to a wrought iron fence that separated the pool deck from an area a few steps down where people could lie in the sun or nap.

After my swim, I'd move Sky to where the hot tub was, hook her leash to the fence there and warm up in the swirling water. The gym is built on an enormous pier that sticks out into the Hudson River. From the hot tub, I could see the boats passing on their way to the ocean and the Statue of Liberty, green and majestic, welcoming all who passed. Much closer to me, I could see Sky. Sometimes just looking at her would cause my body chemistry to change and if I felt poorly, in no time I'd be feeling better.

When I got out of the hot tub, Sky would lead me in reverse back to the locker room and to the shower where I'd put down a towel for her and ask her to wait. There I was dependent on her good will and training. There was nowhere to hook the leash in the shower room. In no time, she had the whole routine nailed, even reminding me with her eyes, should I forget, that when we first got to the locker room, she'd get a cup of water. I was really pleased.

People were used to seeing me at the gym with Flash and knew they should ignore him and let him do his job. But now I was there with a half grown puppy. There were people who couldn't resist trying to pet her. One lady even tried calling her away when I was in the shower and Sky was lying on a towel just outside it. Covered with soap and shampoo, I saw my dog get up and begin to disappear. It must have been quite a sight when I stepped out of the shower, dripping all over the stone floor, to call her back.

If it had been Flash waiting outside the shower, he would have turned his head away when a stranger tried to woo him away. But Sky wasn't even one year old, and learning not to respond to strangers when on the job is one of the more difficult things for service dogs to accomplish. After all, a service dog is still a dog. It's natural for dogs to want pats and kisses wherever they can get them. For working dogs of all kinds, some of the job is natural, based on inborn instincts. Other parts are not. Some, in fact, require the dog to go against his instincts. That's why it takes time and proper training for a dog to learn how to behave when on the job. Sky was doing very well for a young pup. But being enticed was simply more temptation than she was able to resist. That amount of self control would only come with time.

Sky loved going to the gym. I would have thought that waiting for me to swim and shower would be pretty boring for a dog. But that didn't seem to be the case. Perhaps she liked it so much because of the heightened responsibility for my care. It was just the two of us. Steve wasn't there and neither was Flash. It was her show and that made her feel very important. Most of the time, just having her with me made me feel infinitely better than I would feel were I alone. On those occasions when I began to hurt, I'd find a quiet place, sit on the floor and pat my lap, much the way my grandmother did. Because Sky is so little, instead of putting her head in my lap, she put her whole self there, climbing up, curling into a ball and pressing herself against me. Her energy, heat and weight would help my body fend off the pain and in a few minutes, I'd be able to get up and go back to whatever I was doing. Sky knew she had helped me. She could feel my energy change and feel me relax as the pain eased. It's possible, no one knows for sure, that dogs can see auras, the energy field around living things that changes according to mood. If so, she could see that in every way sitting on my lap had made things better. She was very important to me and nowhere was it clearer than when it was just the two of us. Heading for the gym, her tail would wag non-stop. Just watching it wave back and forth like a metronome, if I had one, mine would be wagging, too.

Sometimes a bright idea helps speed the training. The notion to let the kids on the bus pet Sky meant that she learned to like riding on the bus in one trip instead of five or six. One day, leaving the gym, I got another good idea. Sky still hated going in taxis, but it occurred to me that a very short ride ending in a very big treat might change her mind. So even though I love the walk along the river to and from the gym, I began taking a taxi home. We'd get out at the corner of my building, right at an entrance to the little park where Sky loved to play ball. Even before I got out of the cab with her, I had the ball in my hand. After only three cab rides home, Sky started pulling me to the curb. When a cab stopped, she'd get in first. After seeing that, I knew my mission had been accomplished and I decided to walk home. But as soon as we got outside, a car pulled over and stopped to let someone off. In case I wasn't sure I'd solved the problem, Sky pulled me over to the car and tried to hop in.

§§§

When my grandson, Zachary, was a very little boy, I tried to explain to him why he could play with Flash at home but not when we went out to eat and Flash was wearing his service dog cape. I thought I did a masterful job of explaining Flash's job as a service dog and when I finished, just to make sure I'd been clear, I asked Zachary if he'd understood. He said he had. So then I asked him what I'd said. He looked up at me and smiled. "You said Flash was a circus dog."

A year later, I gave it another shot. Once again, I told

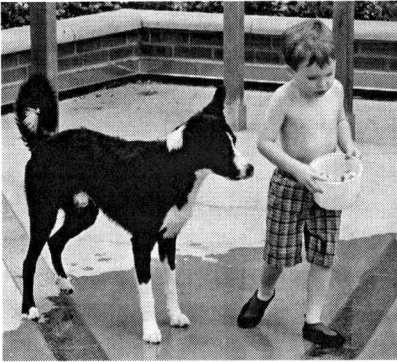

Zachary all about the work my service dog did. He listened carefully. When I finished, I asked if he'd understood. "Yes, Baba," he said. "But *why* is he a nervous dog?"

A nervous dog would not make a good service dog. Service dogs need to be unflappable, calm in the face of whatever comes their way. But a circus dog, now that's another story.

Sky, like her mother, is as agile as an acrobat, as courageous as a lion tamer, as graceful as a bareback rider and, above all, as funny as a clown. After months of playing catch with ducks and then tossing them into the bathtub,

Sky noticed that the tub wasn't the only water in the bathroom. That day, she threw a duck into the toilet and leaned over the edge to watch it bob around in there, delighted with her discovery. A few days later, she improvised on the theme, throwing one of her stuffed animals into the toilet. She was really pleased with herself as she watched it get saturated and sink to the bottom.

In the morning, Sky likes to smother me with kisses, licking my whole face until I squirm away. One day she figured out that if she stood on my hair, I couldn't get away and she could kiss me as long as she liked.

Another time, Sky accidentally put her paw on the button that turned on the radio and, to everyone's surprise, filled the house with music. Some dogs learn from such a mistake. Some don't. Sky did. Now she puts on the radio whenever she thinks a little music would be cheerful.

It turns out that when Zachary was only four, he had the right idea. If laughter is the best medicine, my little circus dog is surely the right service dog for me. Every day I remind myself how lucky I am that the funny little dark tri came to live with me in New York City.

6

§ Denise §

Growing Up Canine: May's Story

As lambing season started winding down, I was able to spend more time with May each day. She would tromp about the house with me, stopping where I stopped, lying down and waiting until I got up to go somewhere else, then following me again, perfectly content to be my quiet little buddy. When outside she could do a 180 degree turn-around from the quiet little house dog and run around with the other dogs like a wild banshee. She could go from one end of the activity spectrum to the other at the drop of a hat. Every once in a while, in between playing or chewing on toys or looking for something to eat, her brown eyes would search mine for a few seconds looking for a connection, and finding one. It was apparent in her everyday activities that she was figuring out what I wanted from her without specific commands and discovering the generalities of how she was expected to behave. She was "getting" me—understanding me.

Like any puppy, she had her naughty moments, particularly chewing on shoes and pillows. However, if I let her know she wasn't allowed to chew on one of my shoes, she figured out that meant all of our shoes were off limits. If we let her know she was not to throw one couch pillow around, she stopped throwing all the pillows around. It was a time of transition

in May's life. At six months old, she was not quite a puppy but not yet an adult. She was trying to settle down and become serious about certain things, but there were plenty of times when she reminded me she was still a puppy.

When a dog is less than six months old, a person can only tell a little about what its temperament will be like as an adult. At about six or seven months, many dogs go through what is called a fear period, where they start to realize things can hurt them, and sometimes this realization causes an exaggerated fear response to things that wouldn't bother them during a different time in their lives. The way a young dog deals with and emerges from this stage can often give the owner a good idea as to what its adult temperament might be like. It's not unheard of for the boldest pup in the litter to come out of this fear period as the most timid, and vise versa. As it turned out, I barely noticed this stage with May. It's possible I was so aware of this fear stage after years of raising puppies that I naturally scaled back on things that could end up being a bad experience for her. Or maybe it wasn't a prominent phase for her. Either way, if she indeed felt any new realization of fear, she must've figured out she could conquer these scary things, because I never noticed her skipping a beat at this age.

Six to seven months is also the age when I like to look at how a pup seems similar to or different from its parents and other relatives I know. Of course, some of these similarities will be good things, and some will be not as good. As an occasional breeder, I want to gather as much information as I can about how traits are passed down— physical traits, personality and social traits, as well as working traits. Naturally, I couldn't tell much about May's working traits yet, but at six months, I could already see some physical and mental similarities to her parents. One thing on the good list was her tremendous athletic ability. While both parents are quite athletic, Kate stands out in her athletic ability. Kate is so light on her feet that she's often air born in a position we call the "Superman pose." May was very fast and agile by six months, and, like Kate, had a

love of being in the air, whether jumping on things or over things.

Like both parents, May has a sweet, fetching personality. With the same warm brown colors on her face, her soft, loving look is just like that of her dad. Also like him, she tries to talk. Unfortunately, some of this need to express herself vocally became problem barking. Aside from the barking, there are a lot of different noises that she makes. Sometimes, when I get after her for barking, instead of stopping altogether, she changes her bark into a different sound instead, a long drawn out "errr." It's certainly a less objectionable noise, and funny, but of course she picks up on my amusement and it eggs her on to continue making odd noises. She's very responsive to particular situations and has an array of sounds that she trots out to use depending on the occasion. If one type sound doesn't work, she switches up and tries another. She has quite a range. Sometimes the sound is soft, like when she's trying to let you know she wants some attention. Sometimes the sound is loud, like when an ambulance goes by with the siren going and May joins right in with a series of high pitched howls. Since she's started doing this, my other dogs have learned to add to her chorus, creating quite a ruckus to my ears. They each have their own vocal variations, so perhaps to them it's like a song where they're all harmonizing in some wolf/doggy way we don't understand. While I think it's hilarious when dogs start howling, I worry that the neighbors don't share my glee and usually quiet them if it goes on too long. Thankfully, most of May's non-barking sounds are soft and expressive. If I had the desire, I think I could teach her to mold her noises into sounds like words. She could be one

of those talking dogs that says phrases like "I ruv ru," like Scooby Doo.

Another mannerism May has that's like her dad's is on occasion when she greets you and is very excited, she "smiles." When dogs smile, which is really just curling their lips up to show you their teeth in a very non-aggressive manner, it's thought to be a submissive gesture. I've only ever known a few dogs that smile, but it always looks like they're just happy to see me, so it makes me smile, too.

Sometimes there are other specific behaviors that get passed down through the generations, such as crossing their front paws a certain way while lying down or picking up food bowls and dragging them to certain areas or even special ways they interact with people or each other. I find it fascinating to note social behaviors that are passed down from parents, grandparents, and even farther back. Most of all, if I've owned or known those dogs the behavior came from, I feel touched as though I'm seeing a little piece of that dog even after it's long gone.

As May reached eight months of age, the lambs were now weaned and had become very interesting little creatures as far as she was concerned. They were not as big and threatening as their moms and they were also quite spritely, running and leaping about, and butting each other in play. I was having a harder and harder time keeping May from watching and trying to work the lambs on the other side of the fence.

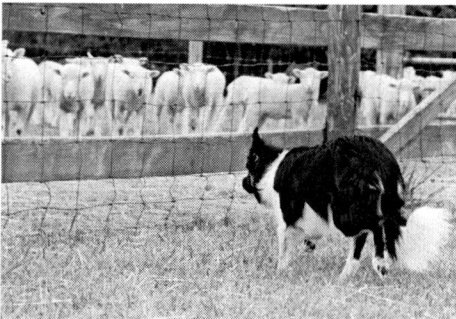

When she was running along the fence trying to work the lambs, she seemed sensible and serious, and also very keen to be in there with them. It became clear it was time to evaluate May on sheep seriously to see if she were ready for training.

The very core of what is bred into a working border collie is the desire to collect livestock and bring it to their person. This instinct is thought to go back to the wolves' hunting packs where members of the pack surround the prey, sometimes forcing it to a stronger wolf for the kill. Only parts of the wolves' instincts to surround and kill prey are useful to humans. Naturally, people don't want their sheep killed. So as the wolf/dog became domesticated, the ones used to help people with their livestock were the ones that respected their humans enough to bring them the stock rather than try to kill them. Essentially, the human replaced the strong wolf pack member.

Other parts of the wolves' hunting instinct were also modified through selecting and breeding only the most useful dogs for humans. While hunting, wolves try to identify the old, sick or young members of a herd as easy targets for their kill. In contrast, a good sheepdog will focus mostly on the strongest sheep or leaders of the herd because those are the sheep it needs to control in order to control the flock. Some sheepdogs are so focused on the adult leaders that they appear not even to see small lambs at all, as if they were invisible. This is the exact opposite of what a wolf would do.

Another way the working-bred border collie differs from the wolf is in the sheepdog's extreme keenness to keep on working, no matter what. In the wild, if game is too hard to catch, the wolf conserves its energy and gives up. A sheepdog that gave up when things got too hard would not be a very useful worker. Therefore, keenness and determination are valued traits in a good working dog.

So the young sheepdog starts its training by using this natural instinct to go around sheep and bring them to or hold them in front of the trainer. This is called balance. The first few sessions are very basic. Using the instinct to hold or bring sheep to their person, the dog should go to and stay on the opposite side of the sheep from the trainer.

When the trainer turns and moves counter-clockwise, the dog circles the same direction in order to balance the sheep in the right place between itself and the trainer.

When the trainer moves in a clockwise direction, the dog will circle clockwise so that it is always across from the handler with the sheep in between them.

If a young dog tries to balance the sheep to the trainer, it shows that it understands the basics of the relationship between itself, the trainer, and the sheep. As the beginner dog refines this instinct for useful work, it develops what is called a *gather*. The first part of the gather is called the *outrun*, where a dog runs out toward the sheep but off to one side in a curved path that looks something like a half of an upside down pear. The dog runs from the person's side and widens this way so it won't disturb the sheep until it gets behind them in a position to bring them more or less straight to the person. Once the dog is behind the sheep in this position, it makes contact with them in what is called the lift. The *lift* is where the dog and sheep check each other out up close. If the dog is confident and determined, the sheep move on in a controlled manner. If the dog is brash or aggressive, the sheep may be difficult to control or try to run away. If the dog is scared or unsure, the sheep may stay where they are and continue to graze, or they may stomp at or butt the dog, trying to make it go away. The lift sets the stage for how easy it is to move and control the sheep during the *fetch*, which is when the dog tries to bring the sheep in a direct path to their person.

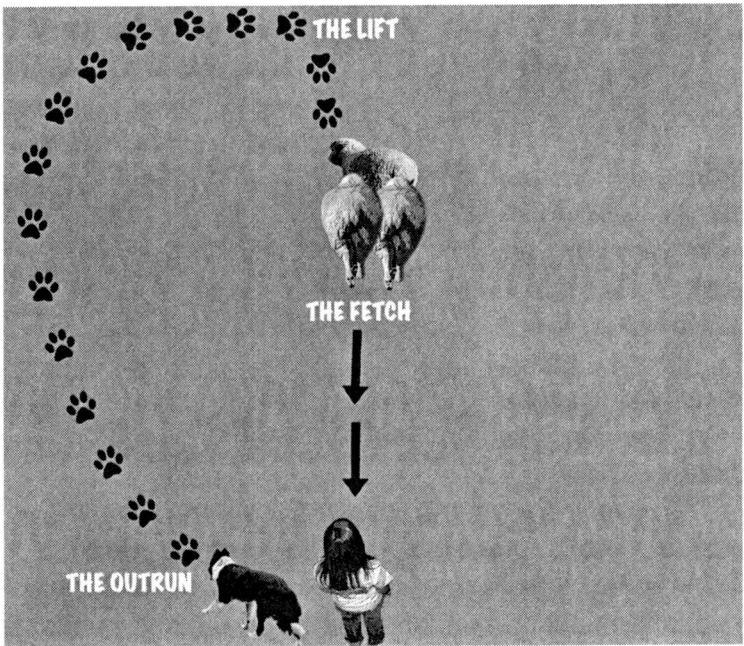

A good, well-trained border collie can gather sheep from a mile away or more. However, in the beginning, most sheepdogs start out their training by going around sheep that are very close to the trainer.

Not all border collies, even strictly working bred ones, will work sheep right off, and some will never work them. In some dogs, the instinct to work develops over time. In others, it can appear quite suddenly. Sometimes, a dog that has never seen sheep or was not mature enough to work before will look as if it has no idea what's going on when first put in with livestock. It wanders around the pen not paying any attention to the sheep, sniffing the ground or eating sheep poop or acting mildly interested in the sheep but not with any good purpose. It may feel somewhat threatened by these strange sheep creatures and try to run away from them or bark at them. Then, in a split second, something miraculous happens. A sheep will dart or move a certain way, and as if the dog has no control over what it's doing, it moves perfectly to control it. People describe this as the light bulb coming on or the dog "turning on." It's always amazing to see this sudden spark of inborn behavior, no matter how many times you see it. Afterward, the dog seems stunned for a second as if it's thinking, "Whoa, what was that!" Once truly "turned on," the dog will usually stay turned on, looking like it always knew what it was supposed to do.

Aside from having the instinct to work, the dog must be keen to work no matter what in order to become useful. No treats or special praise should be needed when training or working a well-bred border collie. Simply being allowed to work is far and away the most important reward for them. The dogs I breed are normally keen to work sheep very early, even as puppies. At six weeks old, Kate squeezed through the fence, ran into the field as fast as her little puppy legs would allow her, and started trying to work sheep with her mom. Like Kate, May was aware of the sheep even as little pup, so there was no defining moment when she suddenly turned on to the sheep. Watching her instinct and keenness develop was a gradual thing. Even though she wanted to work at a young age, and it was tempting to see what she could do, I made myself wait until she was old enough to handle the physical and mental stress of the work and training.

When it was finally time to start May's formal training, a couple of months before she turned one year old, she showed me right off that she did indeed have the inborn desire to go around all of the sheep and bring them to me. She couldn't always do this perfectly, since she was just starting to learn about sheep, but she did have the inborn understanding of what she needed to do, and the desire to try and keep trying no matter what happened. It was important that I recognized when she was trying to do the right thing, even when things didn't go exactly right. Just as even a brilliant first grader is still only a first grader and needs time and experience before being able to do college level work, the young sheepdog needs time to develop all of its instincts and learn how to balance them with self control in order to become a good worker.

I could tell May was thinking the right way from the beginning because her tail was always down. A border collie's tail often shows what kind of attitude it has toward what it's doing. When working stock, a dog with its tail down rather than up in the air over its back or flipping up and down shows the dog has a more serious purpose than just chasing or playing with the sheep.

When I started May's training, I didn't use any commands except a "that'll do" command when we were finished. I also had a somewhat reliable "lie down" command that I occasionally used but didn't drill on. At first, it's more important that the dog learn about sheep and how they react to them than obey specific commands. If the trainer makes good use of body position in relation to the sheep and dog, it should cue instinctive behaviors in a talented young dog. If you can get the dog into the correct position relative to yourself and the sheep, it should make sense to the dog because you're tapping into something already there, however you manage to find the key to unlock it. The trainer can help this process along by making sure the situation and the sheep are not too hard at first so the dog can be successful.

For the first few training sessions, I put May in a small pen with a group of 40–70 older lambs and their mothers. The small pen would help contain the sheep as May developed the basics of how to control them. I used a large number of sheep because the larger the group of sheep, the more they wanted to stay together and the bigger the target for May, making it easier for her to go around all of them as a group. I also wanted her in with enough sheep that if she got frustrated and busted into the middle of the group, as young dogs often do, they would just open up, let her in, then regroup and spit her back out somewhere on the outside of the group again.

The mothers, called ewes, were pretty calm and cooperative, being used to a dog going around them. Sheep used to being worked by dogs are called dogbroke sheep. Lambs, however, tend to panic easily and do unpredictable things. Naturally, the lambs presented a little more of a challenge for May than the dogbroke ewes. Whenever May was too close or too far away or too fast or too slow, or not balancing them correctly, they would take advantage of her inexperience and try to split off from the main group and run away.

However, since they didn't want to get too far away from their moms, they weren't uncontrollable, and they reacted to May in a fresh way that awakened more of her natural instinct to control them. They also brought out a little more frustration in her, since she had to pay more attention to being in the right place in order to keep them from splitting off. I had to watch May's reaction to each situation carefully to make sure she was being challenged enough to develop, but not over-challenged, which could make her lose confidence.

In general, dogs move and control the sheep by either walking straight into them

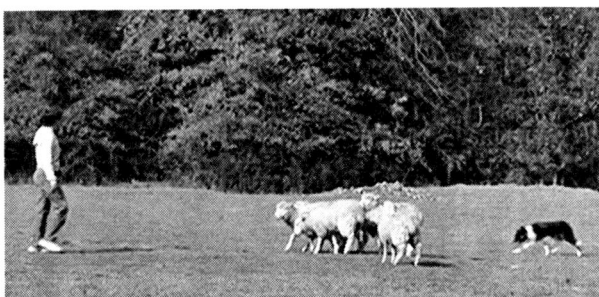

or flanking (moving in a curved path) around them one direction or the other

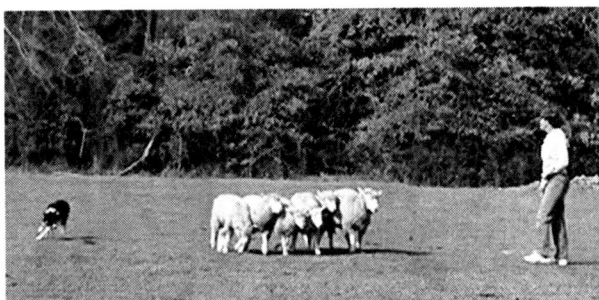

Sometimes the flank will only need to be a few feet in order to change the direction of or control the sheep, and sometimes it will need to cover nearly the distance of a complete circle. Knowing which direction and how far to

flank, how close to be to the sheep, and how fast or slow to go takes talent and experience in both the dog and in the person trying to help the dog. It requires making a judgment about how the sheep will react in each situation. It's not like playing pool where hitting a ball at a certain angle will move it the same way each time. Sheep are living creatures with their own individual emotions and interactions with each other.

Dogs are not all the same either. Just as people write better with their right hand or their left hand, dogs are more coordinated flanking around sheep one direction or the other. When people injure their writing hand and have to switch to writing with the other one, they are clumsy and uncomfortable for a while. As time goes by and they practice, they get better and better at writing with their other hand. May liked to flank around the sheep counterclockwise but was not as good at keeping the sheep together and calm when she flanked clockwise. Like writing with the wrong hand, the more she practiced going in this "bad" direction, the better she would get at it. When she circled around counterclockwise, called her "away to me" flank, she was very comfortable and confident, and she made the sheep comfortable. However, she was clumsy circling clockwise (her "come bye" direction). She would flank too fast and too close because she was uncomfortable and tense. Because of this, she would sometimes get the sheep stirred up, causing the lambs to split off and try to run away. This reaction from the lambs could cause May to become more frustrated, making her want to chase and bite them. But she would need to be able flank well both directions in order to control the sheep. My job was to help her become as skilled and even as she could be in both directions while she was still young and flexible enough mentally and physically to do it.

Sheep work in general can be clumsy starting out, as the dog tries to learn how every movement it makes and even what mood it's in affects the sheep. Sheep sense not only emotions in each other but in other species as well. They never respond in exactly the same way to the actions of the dog or person from moment to moment. Working sheep with a dog is a very dynamic relationship. As time goes by, the dog becomes more able to respond well mentally and physically to the movements of the sheep. The dog also develops what is called feel for the sheep and begins to anticipate what the sheep are going to do even before they do it. At that point, working sheep hopefully becomes more smooth and effortless, where the dog and sheep appear to flow almost as one. The human is also part of this flow. The person directs the dog, but also watches and "listens" to the dog for clues about how the sheep are reacting. A talented, fully trained sheepdog in good partnership with its handler is a beautiful thing to see. Much like the ice skaters or gymnasts at the Olympics, it looks easy but it's not. May and I were a long way from this smooth, natural flow, but I could see bits and pieces of it coming together even through the clumsy times. Even early on, May knew when her work was right. I didn't need to tell her. She felt it when it was right because when the three-way relationship between the handler, dog, and sheep was right, the work was right. Being a part of this mutually respectful relationship is at the genetic core of the working border collie. It is this relationship they are seeking. When we were finished and we'd had a good day with things coming together for her, May would run up to me and leap in the air over and over, as high as she could jump. She knew.

Training is stressful for young dogs, so it's a nice break to let them unwind a bit when we walk in the field each day. Our walks also give the older and retired dogs a chance to exercise and stimulate their minds. There are many things to smell out in the field, apparently different things each day, or even each hour. Dogs can smell things much better than we can. When we walk, my dogs can smell all of the critters that have been in the field for the last few weeks and they can smell how long it's been since they were there. They can smell if intruder dogs have been in the field, and they can tell if they were male or female. Information we gather mostly by seeing and hearing, they find out by using their keen sense of smell, too. Walking through the field and smelling what all has gone on and who all has been there is probably like watching the local news for my dogs. They're always quite keen to investigate each area, no matter how many times they've been over the same ground.

Our field and the woods around it are beautiful in different ways each season, with the fall colors of the trees or the tall grasses blowing in the wind with the sun shining on it just right, or the new green just starting to creep out

in the spring. Sometimes I take a camera in hopes of capturing funny or interesting things the dogs do as they run and play, or for the chance at capturing a special moment in nature.

When I started taking pictures with my camera a few years ago, I found that I began to look for beauty in places I never noticed it before. Now even without the camera, I notice more beauty in the life around me. Like the dogs, I find new and interesting things each day in common places.

The field is a great place for the dogs, young and old, to cut loose and play. Some days they'll all stop abruptly in a circle, look at each other, and then race off together in some game only they know. They play and leap and run then stop suddenly, look at each other, and just as suddenly, off they go again. They never tire of it. Other times they will roll around on the ground playing and tussling until one of them leaps up and runs off, starting a different game of chase me as the others follow. Never are they more excited than when it snows or there's a good mud puddle to splash in. Watching the sheer abandon and joy of life as they play, I feel very lucky to have these wonderful dogs.

The field is also full of dog toys disguised as objects of nature. They find all kinds of things like sticks to throw around and drag, pine cones to toss, or anything little enough to pick up and hoard from the others like some prized possessions. Also, we always have a never-ending supply of rabbits in our pasture. When the weather is warm, there's always an unlucky rabbit or two that gets chased each outing. In all these years, none of the dogs has ever caught one, but the rabbits don't seem to know that and run for all they're worth, zigging and zagging their way to freedom on the other side of the pasture fence before the energetic follower ever catches up to them.

Sometimes on the walks the dogs will stop what they're doing and check in with me, and sometimes one or two will decide to walk with me just to find a little more connection. They each have their own personality with me and their own interactions with each other. Like a human, each dog will have some dogs it is better friends with than others. I often see the same dogs playing with each other each day. Sometimes there are conflicts. Even when their pups are full grown, moms will intervene if they think things are getting out of hand. I once saw Molly break up a rough game between her daughter Kate, then five years old, and Todd, one of the older males. To me, this means they realize they are the mother of that dog, even years later. Things usually stay fairly under control on the walks. I've never found the dogs get too wild if they get out enough and have enough room. At any rate, they get to do pretty much whatever they want in a great big field that for them must be like dog heaven. They're lucky dogs that way.

Dogs appear to learn things—bad and good—from other dogs. They can learn to be afraid of thunderstorms by watching another dog freak out over them. Or they can learn things like coming when called by following other dogs as they come, like May did as a pup. I'm not sure dogs can learn specific trained things like commands from each other when working sheep, but they can learn by tapping into their instincts that go back to the wolves. Wolves will often hunt in packs, surrounding their prey. Even though herding dogs have had their instincts modified to work for humans, they still have an inborn understanding of how to work together to gather the sheep. I've never worked a border collie that wouldn't naturally run out from my side in the opposite direction of another border collie, cross the other dog behind the sheep, and work together to bring them to me. I've even had little puppies naturally do this with an older dog.

As May progressed in her training, I continued to help her develop her gathering skills by gradually increasing the distance I sent her to go around the sheep and bring them to me. As I increased the distance, May started to become a little unsure, sometimes stopping to look at me or running to the sheep very slowly. When that happened, I decided to bring in her mother, Kate. Working with Kate always improved May's confidence. With her mother there, May would run out to the sheep so fast and sure, she looked like she had been shot out of a cannon. She soon sparked right up and figured out she could do it well with or without her mom. She no longer went slow or looked back at me after a few times of running out with Kate. She now had the confidence to go out the length of my field, gather all of the sheep, keep them all together, and bring them to me at a respectful pace. May was over the hump. She had developed the basic gathering skills she was bred to perform.

Next May would need to learn how to do some things that went directly against her inborn instinct to go around sheep and bring them to me. One of these jobs was to drive, which means push the sheep away from me

and sometimes hold them away instead of bringing them toward me. A difficult job where I needed her to drive and hold sheep away was when I put out feed. My sheep are very pushy when they're hungry and wouldn't mind knocking me down and running over me to get to the feed. For my safety, May needed to learn how to keep the sheep from coming near the feed pans while I was putting the feed in. Naturally the sheep were very motivated to outsmart her in this task. They would try to get by her, around her, or sometimes even try to jump over top of her to get to the feed. Since I was busy putting feed out, May had to figure out how to counter each of their attempts to get to the feed before it was time. Luckily, I was able to start her on this new job in the early fall, while there was still some grass. The sheep would fight to get to the feed I was putting out, but not as desperately as they would later in the season when there was nothing else to eat. Consequently, May had some time to hone her new skills and become confident at this new job as the sheep became more and more creative and insistent in getting to the food. Just as people may not have the same amount of self confidence each day, dogs are probably the same. The sheep would test May every day, hoping she would show some weakness they hadn't discovered before. It was how she did over time at this job that would show me how smart, brave, and determined she was. It was quite a challenge for a young dog, but I thought May was up to it.

When sheep get hungry, aside from being very insistent on getting to food, they're pretty good at figuring who's giving it to them. One paddock where I keep the ewes with new lambs is in good view of my kitchen window. Each year, they learn to watch through the windows, hoping to spot me the kitchen. As soon as they see me in the window, they start baaaing as loudly as they can for me to come feed them. Sometimes I won't go into the kitchen for a snack for fear I'll set them off. Once they start, they keep at it until they get fed. Sheep are pretty determined creatures when they're hungry.

It didn't take very many times before the sheep would see me and come running when I went outside to feed with May by my side. When they got close to the feed pans, she would stop them head-on as a group. As they planned their strategy, May watched and waited, alert, crouched down, muscles tense. The mind game began. Many people think sheep are stupid, but they're actually quite intelligent about things important to their own survival, such as getting food. These survival skills have become well-honed over the thousands of years that sheep have been in a prey/predator relationship with other animals. The dogs, too, have honed their senses in order to match wits with their prey. Even though the sheep will not be eaten by the dogs when the dogs work them, they will each use all of the senses they've developed over time. It's a serious interaction, not play, for either species.

It is thought that sheep and dogs can smell emotions in each other. Emotions subtly change the body's biochemistry and thus, its smell. If this is true, then May could tell, perhaps simply by smell, that one of the brave ones was getting up enough confidence to think it could break past her. May would counter that thought with a slight turn of her head toward that sheep or a step sideways and a look that said, "Don't make me come over there." Or maybe May would just hold her ground, and the sheep could tell, possibly by smell, that May was on to her and had the courage to stop her head on if the ewe tried it. The ewe's partners, the other sheep, might get by if May were distracted by her, but the ewe would decide not to be the sacrificial lamb. Next, they might try lining out like football players on one team, with May being the lone player on the other team. She would determine how close the sheep could come to the feed, but no closer, like the line of scrimmage. The sheep on the far end of the line-up might try to break past May, hoping that the sheep on the other end could get by May's imaginary line and the whole defense strategy would fall apart. But May would be swift and determined. She could flank over to the end to stop the offending sheep and still get back in place to stop the whole group in time before they crossed the line.

Then a sheep might stomp at her, hoping to scare her into backing up so they could all get over May's line and get to the feed. But they couldn't intimidate May. She would just put her head down and stare harder at them, giving them a look that said, "Don't mess with me!" The challenging ewe might press May harder, trying to make her lose her patience and bite. But May was smart and didn't spend too much time on any one sheep while the others snuck by. Watching her in these moments, I saw a glimpse of the worker she was to become—brave, determined, confident, patient, quick, and athletic, with the ability to figure out the job at hand, read sheep's intentions, formulate a plan of action on her own, and carry out that plan. May was becoming a real sheepdog.

7

§ Carol §

Conversations With My Dog

If a conversation is a meaningful exchange of information between two individuals, then I had my first conversation with a dog before I had learned how to walk. He was completely white, except for his merry dark eyes and cold, wet, black gumdrop nose. He had long, soft fur, small, thick, pointed stand-up ears, and a plumy tail that he carried jauntily over his back. I don't know who named him—surely not I, because I was months away from uttering my first word. But the name was a natural. Snowflake. In no time, he became my constant companion and some months after he came to live with us, our relationship became a favorite family legend. My parents told the story of me and Snowflake any time they had someone willing to listen. I must have heard it a hundred times.

For the first few months, Snowflake and I grew up together. Wherever I was, he was nearby. He ate the food I dropped, shared my toys, and slept next to the crib or playpen until it was time for us to get busy again. Crawling around the house after him, I probably thought of him as another sibling, one that was a lot more fun than the one I already had. He might have seen me as a littermate of sorts at first. But since dogs mature a lot faster than people, in no time our relationship changed. In order for pack animals, like wolves and their descendants, dogs, to survive, one of the important things they do is to share the responsibility of caring for and protecting their young. Since we were part of the same mixed species pack, it was the most natural thing in the world for Snowflake to begin taking care of me. Being keenly observant, he knew that he could relax when my mother was watching me. But if she turned her back to season the meatloaf or fold the laundry, Snowflake became more alert. When she left the room to answer the telephone, he took over. Best of all, he was there at night, when no one else was. He smelled wonderful, unlike anyone or anything else, so even in the dark, I knew he was there. As far back as I can remember, knowing my dog was nearby made me feel safe.

Eventually, I experimented with standing. It was easier than it might have been because Snowflake would stand next to me, bracing me. When I let go and took my first steps, he stayed right with me. Whenever I fell, as all beginners do, he'd wait patiently for me to get up. If instead I sat there crying, he'd run to get my mother. Without any instructions from human beings, he had it all down to a system.

Like Snowflake, I lived from moment to moment. Babies and dogs don't live in the future or the past. For them, the time is never tomorrow or yesterday. It's always now. So when I was happy, I was as content as it was humanly possible to be. When I was sad, I cried as if my heart had broken into a thousand little pieces, never to be whole again. Snowflake always got the message. Unlike my mother, who liked the smiles, but not so much the tears, Snowflake just accepted what was. To a dog, there are no good emotions and bad emotions. Dogs act on emotions. They don't judge them.

Just as Snowflake understood me, I came to understand him. Soon enough, without any words, we were communicating pretty well. Since neither of us could speak, there were no verbal misunderstandings so common among humans. Instead, we had a meeting of the minds that felt more comfortable and complete to me than what I felt with the other members of my family. They always wanted things, things I was not always able to deliver. Snowflake showed me early on that mistakes were inevitable, that not everyone cared about the same things and that a dog's love is not dependent upon any particular achievements. On good days and bad, a dog will love you anyway. Growing up, whatever I felt, whatever gibberish I "talked," Snowflake understood. When he play-bowed, curled up in a corner or looked longingly at the cookie I was gumming, I understood. And so our conversations went.

It's no wonder, with Snowflake as a nanny, that I became completely obsessed with dogs. When I was about ten, I decided I'd become a dog trainer when I grew up. Many years later, when that finally happened, I named my dog school "Oliver and Me." Oliver was my Golden Retriever.

Ollie and I would train dogs on their own turf. He would wait in the car while I would teach the dogs how to do the things their people needed them to do—come when called, walk nicely on a leash, sit to greet people—and not to do the things their people didn't want them to do—chew the living room rug, bark at the mailman, go to the bathroom in the house instead of outdoors. At each lesson, Ollie's job was to make sure the dog would work even when there was another dog nearby. He was what is called "a distraction

dog." Once my student knew what "sit" meant and would do it when asked to, I'd bring Ollie out of the car. While the dog's person held the leash and the dog did his sit, Ollie and I would walk a big circle around them or I would ask Ollie to sit nearby. Once the new student would sit with another dog around, I knew he understood what to do much better than if he only obeyed the command while in his own living room where everything was familiar and there were no distractions. I loved being a dog trainer. As for Ollie, I don't know if he appreciated top billing, but I know he loved his job, too. All I had to do was pick up my car keys and he'd be at the front door, waiting, his tail wagging a mile a minute.

Now I was not only having conversations with my own dog, but with other people's dogs as well. Sometimes the conversation was as simple as it gets. I'd show a dog what I wanted, I'd ask the dog to do it, he'd do it. The conversation might look like this:

Me: Sit
Dog: You got it!
Me: Good dog. Thanks!

Only the dog didn't say his part out loud.
Sometimes the conversation went differently.

Me: Sit
Dog: I don't think so!
Me: Watch carefully. I'll show you again what I mean when I say "sit."

This time, had you been there, the only word you would have heard was "sit." Nonetheless, both the dog and I understood each other. He felt it was important to stay in control. I knew from experience that even the most reluctant student comes to love getting trained. All dogs love the chance to use their minds. And between humans and animals, most things get accomplished without words.

Dogs don't really need a spoken language to let us know what's on their minds. For one thing, they use the same body language as wolves to communicate among their own kind and with our species as well. They bow down with their rumps in the air to invite play, tuck their tails and round their backs when they are afraid, put their ears forward, raise their hackles (the hair that runs down their backs) and stand on their toes to look bigger and more fierce when they are angry, and when they are as happy as it is possible to be, they have an open laugh-y mouth, a held-high wagging tail, and they wiggle.

Dogs also "speak" with their eyes. When a dog gazes at you with his round, brown eyes, he is expressing undying love. Or the desire to share your ice cream cone. Or he's telling you his water bowl is empty, especially if he looks into your eyes, looks at his water bowl, then looks at you again.

Looking softly into a dog's eyes, even when he doesn't look from you to his water bowl, you can often know what he is feeling or thinking. The more you look, the more you see. You can see if he's happy or sad. You can see if he's feeling stressed or if something is hurting him. You can see when he thinks now would be the perfect time to play. You can see just about everything you might need to know. Like us, dogs think in pictures and sometimes, I have no idea how, you can even see the picture the dog is imagining.

This works the other way around as well. When dogs look at us, they know how we feel, just the way Snowflake knew how I felt when I was little, and now, many years later, Sky knows. They seem to know what we are thinking, too, and what our intentions are. Long before I pick up a leash, my dogs know we're going for a walk.

They know when I'm about to stop working, sometimes even before I do. Without a word on my part, they know when I'm pleased or not at something they have done. They read body language, breathing patterns, messages in our eyes. Often, it seems, they can read our minds. Maybe *they* can see the pictures we form in *our* minds. Maybe we picture going for a walk, for example, long before we pick up the leash.

This kind of conversation, understanding each other without a word, is the basis of friendship and training; for Sky, it is the foundation of her life as a service dog. By one year of age, Sky would toss the ducks back into the bathtub without first beheading them (Did I forget to mention that part?), she could take food I offered her from a fork or chopsticks, she would lie down, if asked to, half way back from fetching a ball, and when I shook my head and growled, she would pick up a toy and do the same, the dumbest and funniest trick I'd ever taught a dog in my life. She was also progressing as a service dog.

When it was time to go out, I was the one who decided which dog I would take. In the house, it was often another story. Sky was still learning what to do by copying Flash. For his part, when she began to step up with any regularity, he made himself scarce. But despite the fact that the work was getting more difficult for him, despite the fact that he needed more rest and quiet time than he had years earlier, he found it hard to let go of his life's work. Every dog yearns to be a contributing member of his family. That's part of his heritage, passed down through time from his wolf ancestors. Just because Flash was old didn't mean he was ready to quit. He had always done his job with enormous passion, and sometimes it seemed to me that he was thinking about his job and how he could do it better even when he wasn't working, the way a person might. Now that Sky was coming up on the bed and lying against me, doing "keppie," it would seem that Flash might be happy, even grateful, that he could go off quietly by himself and have a much deserved break. Yet that's not what happened. When I would need to lie down and wait for pain to diminish, it was Sky who joined me, pressing close and kissing me in her own enthusiastic style. Flash would disappear, but often he'd come right back with a toy in his mouth. At twelve, no toy could have distracted Flash from doing his job. But Sky wasn't twelve. She wasn't even two yet. The moment he showed up, bit down on the toy to make it squeak and danced around in his "let's play" mode, she was gone. He would woo her away and off they'd race to the living room to play tug of war or catch-me-if-you-can and there I'd be, all alone. I wouldn't have thought a dog could be of two minds about something. I thought that was only a human thing. But I was wrong. Not being a kid any more myself, I understood Flash's feelings completely. There was no way I would interfere. I knew, as time went by, he'd let Sky work more and more. He really needed her to, as did I. I knew that as she matured, Sky would be more able to concentrate on working and get more and more satisfaction from doing so. For now, I would accept the help that was given and not ask something unfair from either dog.

Lying in bed, listening to Sky and Flash playing helped me, too. Their joy was infectious and their energy filled the house. Often, I'd fall asleep for a while and when I woke up, either Sky or Flash would be lying next to me. If I were really lucky, both dogs would be there. That's when I was happiest, when I was squashed in the middle of a dog sandwich.

I still took Flash out with me sometimes. I wanted to see the light in his eyes when I picked up his cape, and I always felt so safe when I was with Flash. But sometime during his twelfth year, I became limited in where I could take him. He would occasionally have an accident, peeing someplace where that wasn't a very good idea. I decided to take him to a specialist. After a lot of tests, I was told he had early kidney disease. That only meant more walks for Flash. He wasn't in pain, and I was assured that he had several good years left. I cried all the way home. A few good years would mean he'd live to be a very old dog, but I couldn't stand the idea that anything was wrong with him.

Every morning I'd take the dogs out to play in the courtyard in back of the building where we live. I'd take two balls with me so that they could both retrieve without competing—by now Sky was fast enough to get every throw if there were only one ball. I threw the ball farther for her since she was young and her energy was over the top. Sky was fast and strong and I loved to watch her run. But it was Flash running that made my heart pound. He was bigger and taller and longer than she was. When he went full tilt, stretching his body out, reaching with his long legs, he was as graceful as a jungle cat. I think watching my dogs run and play was as glorious for me as it was for them. After a run and a nice long walk around the Village, Flash would need a long nap and he'd disappear. Sky would stay with me while I worked on my current book, sleeping near the desk so that she wouldn't miss me getting up, even if I were just going to the kitchen for a snack.

Little by little, Sky was figuring out when and how to help me. When she got a small part of it, no matter how small, I'd praise her to let her know she was on the right track. Sometimes I'd praise her with words, the way I'd praise a speedy, cheerful response to "Sky, come!" I'd tell her "Good keppie" and listen for the happy thump of her tail on the bed. Other times, when she'd flop down beside me and sigh, I'd sigh back to her. Using her language in addition to mine meant I had shortcuts, quick and easy ways to let her know she was on the right page without a lot of unnecessary lip flapping. Dogs are the world's best listeners. You can tell them all your secrets and unlike some humans, they'll never reveal a word to anyone. But it's nice, too, to be able to communicate without talking. When Sky sighed, I knew she was aware she was working, that she wasn't there at my side only because it felt good to her. When she sneezed, it meant she was happy. I'd sneeze back. Sometimes we'd just hang out together without a word or a sound. Being together made us both feel calm and safe. Often I'd stop in the middle of a walk and find someplace to sit. A favorite spot was a bench facing the Hudson River. She'd hop up and lean against me. We'd sit there quietly looking out over the river until either one of us decided it was time to go.

It wasn't unusual for Sky, and Flash before her, and Dexter before him, to comfort me by leaning against me. Wolves and domestic dogs alike keep their puppies warm with the heat of their own bodies. It's a way that they insure the future of their packs or families. It's about survival. There was nothing deeper, more satisfying or more natural for Sky to do than to take care of me and during her second year, she understood that. Of course, it was a mutual thing. I took care of her, too, not only by feeding her the very best food I could afford, by making sure she had plenty of exercise for her body and her mind, and by providing her with a clean, dry, warm place to sleep—my own bed—but petting her and leaning against her gave her comfort, too. Instead of feeling isolated because she lived in a city instead of in the country like her sister May and because she lived with a small, mixed species pack instead of with a large group of dogs, Sky felt connected. She did work she now understood was important. And she had a person who loved her to the moon and back. Like many people with illnesses that don't go away, I felt different in a bad way. But instead of feeling isolated, as I used to before I had my first service dog, I, too, felt connected. The intimate relationship between my dog and myself gave me back what having a disability took away. It seemed to put me back on an even footing with everyone else. Instead of feeling alone, with Sky at my side I felt part of the human race, ready to face anything, even when I was ill. There's no prescription, no man-made pill that can do what a dog can do. Sitting and watching the river with Sky, I knew how lucky I was.

Denise was sending me lots of pictures of May and sheep. I sent her pictures, too, of Sky playing ball or playing with Flash or looking up at the camera with her sweet face. I sent lots of pictures of Sky playing with my grandchildren, sitting in a field of flowers, and chewing on a bone.

But there were no pictures of Sky working because even if there were, no one would have an idea what she was doing.

When someone can't see and is being led by a dog, it's easy to understand why the person needs help and what the dog is doing. Or if someone is in a wheelchair and the dog is helping to pull the chair, or opening a door for the person, or fetching something the person dropped, that's easy to understand as well. But when you can't see what's wrong with a person, when the disability is probably something you never heard of in the first place, how could you possibly know that a service dog is helping? Disabilities that don't reveal themselves to the casual observer are called "invisible disabilities." But they are not invisible to dogs.

Service dogs who help with invisible disabilities seem to be doing magic because in most cases, we humans don't understand how they know there's a problem. Since we can't just look at someone and know they are in pain, we are simply amazed that dogs know these things and can respond to their partners in a helping, sometimes life saving, way.

Some people think that dogs can diagnose what's wrong with us by using their powerful sense of smell. We surely know that they can analyze scents—just think of their marking behavior. Other people think dogs have some kind of sixth sense that lets them know there's trouble brewing. Maybe they can hear our heartbeats which might speed up if something's amiss. Or perhaps our breathing patterns change—we breathe faster or more shallowly. No one knows for sure. What we do know is that wolves know which prey animals are sick, weak, or lame and that ability is a trait that domestic dogs have inherited. Wolves use this skill to help themselves survive. Dogs use it to help each other, but also to help us.

While Sky's work may not look like work, watching to see when your partner is in trouble is a really hard job. It takes a lot of concentration. As Sky began to understand her job better, she began to understand *why* she was doing the things she had copied from Flash. Now she wasn't only at my side because she'd seen Flash do that or because I'd pet her and kiss her when she came to be with me. Now she knew when I was hurting. She'd stay longer. She'd keep her tail low. Even her eyes looked more serious. As she began to understand her job the way Flash did, she needed activities that would help her to get rid of the stress she felt knowing that the person she loved most in the world was in pain.

I always tried to play with Sky every day, no matter what. Once in a while, we all needed to relax in a bigger way. The February after she turned one year old, we packed our bags and flew down to Florida to visit our grandchildren. Living in a big city where the law required dogs to be on leash in most places, there was nowhere to

teach Sky how to chase and catch a Frisbee. But across the street from where my grand-kids lived, there was a grassy hill, left untouched because it was too steep to build a house on. It was the perfect place for three kids and a more-than-willing collie to begin a game of Frisbee.

When we were in the house, Sky usually seemed to understand which of the fifty or so toys in the family room were dog toys and which were kid toys, not to be touched. At dinner, she hung around Abby, the youngest, who dropped the most food on the floor. And when she was so tired she could no longer keep her eyes open, she slept in the middle of everything, not wanting to miss a minute away from the kids even when she was sleeping.

Back at home, our friend Phil was staying with Flash. Flash could no longer navigate an airport without an accident. Staying home with good company seemed the best solution. During the day, Phil walked Flash often. At night, they slept side by side. Flash adored Phil so he was having a little vacation, too.

For Sky, school was never out. At home or away, I was ready to use any opportunity to further her education because I knew that the more she was taught, the faster and better she would learn. So teaching her anything—even catching a Frisbee—was valuable. Unexpected problems come up all the time for service dogs and their partners and sometimes, they have to be solved on the spot. By seeing to it that Sky was a quick study, I was doing the best I could to make sure that when obstacles arose, we could overcome them. Sometimes that meant that Sky would have to generalize. If cars, taxis and buses are okay, then trains and boats should be okay, too. Other times it might mean teaching Sky something new right then and there—to back up into a small space, to lie halfway under a chair, to refrain from wiggling when she was lifted up because the fastest way out of an airport meant riding on an escalator.

Unlike guide dogs who are taught to notice things way overhead—like tree branches—that might harm their much taller human partners, or mobility dogs who open doors with a special gadget for their partners in wheelchairs, Sky couldn't be trained by someone else. She was learning her job by being with me. You can't teach a dog to know when you're in pain any more than you can teach a dog to know when a seizure is coming, when someone's blood sugar is too low, or when someone needs to take heart medication pronto. Being with their human 24/7, dogs will begin to notice these things and to take responsibility for them. It sounds amazing, but it's pretty much normal behavior for a dog, making sure the pack survives. Away from home, a service dog will be even more attentive to her partner. Sky already knew that when it was just the two of us, she needed to watch more carefully, the same way Snowflake did when my mother didn't have her full attention on me. She would be more serious and alert when Steve wasn't with us. But even when he was, when we visited our grandchildren or spent the weekend with Richard and Polly, she always seemed clearer about her work and more dedicated by the time we got home.

Of course, when we were in the country with her friend, Nellie, you might not have thought Sky was a service dog at all.

She and Nellie ran free, swimming in the pond, racing around the house, wrestling toys out of each other's mouths, and playing Nellie's favorite game. Here's how it went. Nellie would snag a ball, hide it—often in plain sight—then get behind a tree, a bush, a sprig of grass, and tremble with anticipation waiting for Richard or Polly to find the ball and throw it for her.

Sometimes she'd grab the ball just as they reached for it. Or if they failed to see it, she might stare into their eyes as if trying to send them the secret location. If that failed, she'd grab the ball herself, hide it again and start the game anew. The first time she played the game in front of Sky, Sky

merely grabbed the ball and pranced off with it.

Nellie couldn't *believe* that Sky didn't know the rules of the game—so she proceeded to teach them to her. After that, there'd be two balls in play and two dogs hiding, waiting for some human to discover the balls and throw them as far as possible. They played on the grass. They played on the deck. Funniest of all, they played in the pond, hiding the ball at the very edge and then waiting in the water, just their heads sticking out among the reeds.

Of course Sky, having stolen the ball from Nellie, knew the consequences of letting go—so she didn't.

Despite the endless fun to be had when she was in the country, Sky would always come to find me and see how I was. Once or twice over the weekend I'd take her out alone. We'd walk up the hill or over to a neighbor's land. I didn't use a leash or give any commands. We just spent a little time alone together because that was an important part of our everyday lives. No matter how much fun she had in the country, Sky always seemed happy to be home again. Even after only two days away, she always came back refreshed, working better than ever.

During the spring of that year, Flash was still working, but mostly when he felt he could. He still played ball and he still played with Sky several times a day. At this point in Flash's life, he didn't initiate the play. Sky did that. She would start by bringing him a toy. If he didn't respond, she'd bring another and another and another, as if giving him an array to choose from. When that didn't get a rise out of Flash, she'd lie on her back, roll around and make the most amazing sounds, barks, yips, whines, pleading for him to join her in a game. If all else failed, she'd stand in front of him, lift one front paw and smack him in the head. It wasn't a human smack. It was a little puppy smack, one that said, "C'mon, let's play." It always did the trick. He'd be up and after her in a game of racing through the house, over the furniture and, when it was warm enough to leave the door open, out into the garden and back. It seemed that Sky was the best medicine not only for me, but for our old boy as well.

As spring became summer and Sky got better and better at her job, I tried to keep up as many of Flash's routines as possible. We almost always started the day in the back courtyard, playing ball before we took a walk. This was fun for the dogs but also self-preservation for me. Collies are fast and reactive dogs. If I didn't let them use up some of their exuberant energy, it would be really hard to walk them together. One August day, as usual, I brought out two balls so that Sky could go after one and Flash could snag the other. I tossed one ball for Sky and the other, not as far, for Flash. Flash began to run and suddenly fell. He got up right away but I noticed that he'd scraped one front leg and it was bleeding. He paid no attention at all to his leg. He was only interested in getting the ball. He brought it back and I tossed it again, but only a few feet, just to make sure he was okay. Then we went for a long walk around the neighborhood and when we came back home, I put some antibiotic on his scrape and went to my desk to start working.

We had a pretty normal day. The dogs ate a big breakfast, played and napped off and on during the day, went for a big walk in the afternoon and came on the bed to cuddle while we watched TV at night. But when Steve took Flash out for the last walk of the day, Flash fell twice. The first time, he got up and continued walking. The second time, he couldn't get up and Steve had to carry him home.

We took Flash to our veterinarian the next day and stood mute looking at the x-ray of his spine, which was completely deformed by arthritis. It wasn't a wonder that he fell. It was barely believable that he could still walk at all. Dogs are notorious for not showing pain. Until this point, people thought Flash was still in his prime, six or seven perhaps, still vital and strong. He'd had us all fooled. For a few days, Flash lay on soft towels near the door to the garden. We hoped for a miracle but instead, he only got worse. He couldn't get up. Though I cooked for him and offered him warm food from my hand, he wouldn't eat a bite. In fact, he was so miserable, he wouldn't look at any of us.

Sky brought him every toy in the house, placing them carefully in front of him. Then she lay on her back and wiggled around, making her funny, pleading sounds and trying to catch his eye. Finally, she got up and gave him a puppy smack. That had always worked for her, until now.

Baffled, she lay down at his side, the way she did with me when I was in pain, sighed and stayed a long, long time.

When Sky got up, it was my turn. I lay down next to Flash the way he'd always done with me. For years, he'd helped me function better. He'd made it so that I could be part of the world instead of staying home sick. Though I tried to thank him, there were no words that could come close to expressing my gratitude for all he had done for me. So, like Sky, I stayed close to him for a long, long time, feeling the heat of his body against mine for the last time. Working dogs make poor invalids. Flash was as miserable as I'd ever seen a dog. Later that day, we took him back to the vet so that he could be helped out of harm's way.

He'd been to Paris twice where he'd played ball near the Eiffel Tower,

eaten thick, rich French yogurt for breakfast, and been treated like royalty wherever we went. He'd been to Seattle in the rain (you can hardly be in Seattle any other way) and to San Francisco where he rode on a ferry—and loved it—and barked back at the sea lions in San Francisco Bay. He had been my lifeline, my constant companion, my very best friend. When we lost him the summer before he would have turned thirteen, the three of us were absolutely devastated, but none more than Sky.

With her mentor, model of behavior and best buddy gone, Sky stepped up yet again. Now it was her job, and her job alone, to take care of me, and that she did with increasing accuracy and dedication. She also became the guardian of the front door, the greeter of all guests and my too constant playmate. As much as I played with her, it was never enough. I hadn't realized exactly how much energy Flash and Sky used up in their game playing. It was evidently much more than I knew. Now Sky and I played more ball outside, stayed out longer and longer on walks and excursions, thought up places to go that required a long walk to get to and played games from bed when I was too tired to get up. Even at ten o'clock at night, Sky was lobbing balls at me. She was not only lonely. She was getting weird. I knew she needed to play with other dogs and made dates for her in the back courtyard, but none of it was what she was missing, and I surely understood. Every place we looked, Flash wasn't there. No matter what we did, the house seemed too empty, too quiet, and too sad.

We decided to go away. We thought if we were somewhere where we had never been with Flash, we wouldn't keep waiting to hear his footsteps coming down the hall the way we did at home. We thought that if we were away, we wouldn't miss him quite as much.

We had heard that Nova Scotia was one of the most beautiful places on earth. There we could walk on beaches, see waterfalls and hike endless miles of natural trails, and maybe even see a moose but hopefully not run into a bear. Being out of doors and active seemed just the ticket for all of us.

The flight was short, under three hours, and Sky took care of me while we were in the air. She navigated the airports with ease. By now, she was an old pro at traveling. For the first few days, we stayed in Halifax, the capital, spending one of those days driving around the city and going to dog parks with our Canadian friend Jamie, and his dog Misty, a Cairn terrier. The next day, Ryan, our guide, picked us up in his van, and we headed north, to Cape Breton. I'd asked Ryan if we could stop at a beach every day so that Sky could run and he took the request seriously. In fact, though it was chilly enough for a heavy sweater under a windbreaker, he loved eating out of doors and planned on picnic lunches every day. Our first was on a beach and while Sky ran and ran and ran, playing with the ocean waves, smelling shells and bird tracks, I sat on a log shivering and eating a turkey sandwich. When she decided to go exploring, heading down the beach, I got up and followed, glad for the chance to move around and warm up.

We'd decided not to let Sky go swimming and then get Ryan's van soaking wet, but when I came around a bend in the land where Sky, running ahead of me, had disappeared, I saw that the ocean had made an inlet across the sand and formed a serene and beautiful lagoon. In the lagoon, there was my pretty little border collie swimming. Since she was already as wet as she could possibly be, I didn't see any harm in tossing a piece of driftwood for her to retrieve.

When we got back to where Steve and Ryan were sitting, Ryan took a look at Sky and started to laugh. Every day after that, no matter how cold it was, we ate lunch out of doors, and every time we were near the ocean, a river or a bay, Sky went swimming. Wherever there was water, there was Sky, as happy as could be.

We hiked through glades of trees, across small wooden bridges, up and down rocks and across streams to find hidden waterfalls. We walked in wet sand until our shoes made a sucking sound and it was hard to lift our feet to go forward. On the muddiest beach, Sky sank up to her ankles and was so excited, she jumped all over the three of us, leaving muddy footprints on all our clothes, making us laugh and laugh. We went on two whale tours and while we were a little too late in the season for whales, a school of dolphins followed our boat, leaping out of the water in twos and threes and staying with us until we headed back to shore.

At night we went to listen to local musicians play. Sky would lie next to my chair, often resting her head on my foot the way she did in the movies. But at one place, she could see people milling about outside through the oversized window behind our table and she woofed once. Border collies are bred to be aware of movement, big and small, and every little sound. That's one of the things that helps them work sheep so skillfully. But we weren't in a meadow. We were in a pub, and I was very embarrassed that she'd barked. When one of the musicians asked if there was a dog there, I sheepishly raised my hand. Instead of being annoyed, the musician joined us during his break, and when we left after the next set, he followed us out. We sat on the steps of the wooden porch and he told us his dog had just died. We told him we'd lost one, too. Then we sat there quietly, his hand on Sky, until his break was over.

We were really busy during the day.

It was mostly at night, when things got quiet, that I thought about Flash. We used to sleep like spoons, my body against his warm back. Sky did that, too, but she also had her own innovation. She liked to face me. Every night while we were away, she'd lie on the bed, gazing at me with the kind of undying love you can only get from a dog.

If I had some pain, she'd reach out and put her paw right on it. I was surprised how hot her paw was and how precise she was about finding the spot that needed her help. I'd shut off the light and with Sky's face just inches from mine and her warm, little paw against me, I'd fall asleep. If I woke up in the middle of the night, even if Sky was no longer touching me, I could smell her and knew she was close by. As it always had, it made me feel safe.

8

§ Denise §

A Useful Dog

How did we ever get from this:

to *this*?

As I watched May grow and mature, I often looked back on my life and how I came to appreciate a good working border collie.

When I was a little girl, my parents, my younger sister, Robyn, and I lived in a small house in Greensboro, North Carolina, about forty-five minutes from the farm where I live today. In my preschool years we always had cats. I loved the cats, but I was really drawn to my grandmother's dogs. Happily, I spent several days a week at my grandparents' farm. It was only a few miles away from where we lived, but it was a different world.

My grandmother owned and bred working border collies. She only had one at a time. They were always female, always rough-coated, tri-colored, and they were all named Dolly. There were probably four or five serial Dollys from my early childhood until my grandmother died. She got them as puppies, and they lived out their lives on the farm, having perhaps two or three well-planned litters along the way. All the Dollys were from the best working bloodlines at the time from both the US and overseas. Back then there weren't many pet border collies. They were almost all working bred. My dad told me that as far back as he could recall they had farm collies for farm work that looked like border collies. He didn't remember their names but I bet they were all named Dolly, too.

My grandmother never formally trained any of her dogs, but because of their good breeding, they probably didn't need much training to do their jobs. They learned the chores of the farm and they did them. Back when my dad was a kid in the 1930s, everybody, man, woman, or dog, was expected to pull his or her weight, and no one thought it a big deal when a smart dog figured out and did its part. That was just the way it was. By the time I came along, my grandparents no longer had any livestock but they still had the dogs.

My earliest memory of one of my grandmother's dogs was sitting on the screened-in porch one evening after supper while the then-current Dolly had puppies. It took a while, but my grandmother, my mother, and I sat on the porch and watched until the last of the five fat, screaming, wiggling puppies was delivered, cleaned off and nursing. Afterwards, I made sure I was at my grandmother's house nearly every day playing with the puppies as they grew. They looked like furry little bears except for the characteristic border collie blaze on their faces. They loved playing with me, and I sure loved playing with them. What kid wouldn't? I so wished I could have one but my mother said no, our house and yard were too small.

Finally, after several years and a couple more litters with me begging for a puppy each time, we moved to a bigger house and I finally got my puppy. She was black and white with a snip of white on the tip her nose instead of a blaze. We named her Cinder. And so my own journey with border collies began, long before they were the household name they are now.

Today, if you mention border collies to the average person on the street, they'll usually say, "Oh yeah, those smart dogs." And smart they are. Cinder picked up what we wanted her to do and fit in with family life with little problem. Looking back, we never actually trained her, but she figured out much of what we wanted on her own. We would say things like, "Cinder, go wake up daddy," and Cinder would run back to the right bedroom, put her head on the bed, and lick my dad in the face until he woke up. Even in our non-sheep-owning household, Cinder found a little work to do. This is not to imply that all border collies automatically become the perfect pets. They surely don't. Often, when left to their own devices and without enough to do, they can become mischievous or even destructive. We were lucky. But then again, Cinder was bred from top working lines. These were dogs bred to read even very subtle cues that indicated the intentions of sheep. They were bred to work with people to do what the person wanted to control the sheep. It wouldn't be a stretch to imagine that they used some of their sheep reading skills to read what their people wanted from them without the people even having to ask.

We never worked Cinder on sheep ourselves, but we did take her out to a local sheepdog trainer to let him work her. He seemed very pleased with how well she did on his flock of sheep. He told us her good breeding showed.

Now, many years and border collies later, I was expecting yet another dog, May, to read my mind and figure out how to act. I was expecting more from dogs now, but I had gotten better at helping my dogs read me. I had also gotten better at reading them. Over the years, I learned various things that I could do with my body that would translate into some sort of signal, or language to the dogs. Much of this body language is universal. It's something every dog can understand. Soon enough, this became the way I wanted to interact with all my dogs. I wanted to "be" with them in a way they understood naturally, a way that made it easier for every new dog to learn what it was I wanted it to do. I was careful not to ask a dog to do one thing while my body language might be telling it to do the opposite. A good example is one I mentioned before: If you sit on the ground, you're giving the dog a natural signal to come and jump all over you. If you watch dogs together, when a dominant dog lies down, the other dogs will come and glom all over it, licking its face and jumping on top of it, and the dog doesn't seem to mind. This is especially true if the other dogs are puppies. This behavior can even be seen in wolf packs.

So when I decide to sit on the ground and a bunch of dogs are out, I don't try to teach them not to bug me or not to glom all over me. I realize that my actions have given them a natural signal that all dogs understand—it's okay to pile on the human! On the other hand, if I'm working my dogs or simply not in the mood to be jumped on, I don't sit on the ground. In the same way that dogs behave with each other, I try not to give mixed messages. Instead, I use body language when I can to cue whatever it is I want or will allow the dogs to do.

There are many natural signals trainers give to dogs when working sheep, too. One is the body pressure we put on dogs at first when we step toward them to push them away from us and encourage them to go to around to the opposite side of the sheep in order to balance the sheep to us. For the first few months of training on sheep, I don't do much that betrays these natural signals. During this time, the young dog learns to trust me and a partnership bond starts forming. What I'm asking it to do makes sense because it's merely refining what has been bred into it as a sheepdog. But not all jobs on sheep are things that are natural for the dogs to do. Even then, I'm able to use body signals to help my dogs learn what it is I need them to do. These signals can be very subtle, sometimes as subtle as looking at a sheep you want the dog to hold in place, and the dog will understand.

Border collies are also bred to be problem solvers. Many of them will try to understand the job you're trying to do with the sheep instead of just concentrating on the individual steps. Once they can see the end point, or the purpose of the job, they can figure out how to help in their own way. This is what happened when May discovered ways to keep the sheep away while I put out feed. Some dogs are more focused on the job than others, just as some people are more independent thinkers and some need to be told what to do. May, as it was turning out, was very focused on the job, much like her grandmother, Molly.

Most things that dogs do for people are based on a simple system of one action or behavior that results in a reward if it's correct. Sheepdogs often need to carry out a number of complicated actions in order to do a job. They don't work using a simple reward system like one you would use to teach a dog a trick. They need to understand a general goal and be flexible and inventive to do whatever it takes to reach that goal. May's understanding of the job was so complex that if she were doing a job she already understood but doing it incorrectly, I could call her over to me and talk to her a little in a disapproving voice. Then I'd send her back to work, expecting that she would understand she needed to do better, and she usually would. A working dog's attitude is at least as important as their inborn talent.

The winter after May turned one year old, she began helping me with quite a few of the barn chores. With each new job, it would only take her a time or two of doing it before she understood what to do. She would hold sheep off feed or take them out to another field while I put out feed.

She had also learned to drive the sheep down to a chute where I wormed or vaccinated them. She could hold the group quietly in a corner, not letting any escape while I caught and treated sick sheep or trimmed hooves that had grown too long. In this situation, my attention was on the sheep I wanted to catch and hold, not the main group. May had to understand what I was doing and help me catch the sheep. Once caught, she needed to redirect her attention and not be distracted while she held the rest of the group together but away from me and the sheep I was treating.

When it came time to shear the wool off the sheep in the spring, a good dog can prove invaluable. May helped gather and sort the sheep quickly and efficiently so the shearer could work at a steady pace without having to wait for the next sheep that needed shearing.

May was learning how the sheep on our farm responded to her in each situation. All sheep are not the same. Different breeds have different charac-teristics that make them suitable for different parts of the country and various types of livestock operations. Sheep's main defense against danger is to flock together in a tight group. In numbers, sheep feel safe. It is said that a sheep does not act like a normal sheep unless it has at least two other sheep with it. They're even more stable if there are at least four in the group. The need for others in the flock is so strong that a single sick sheep, taken away from its flock, may become worse or even die from the additional stress of being alone. Much of sheep's behavior and instincts are directed toward flock dynamics. The saying "sacrificial lamb" is a real instinct in sheep. In a situation where the group is threatened enough, one sheep, and it instinctively knows which one it is, will break off from the others and run in a different direction. This action is an attempt to persuade the perceived predator to go after the vulnerable lone sheep while the rest of the flock is saved.

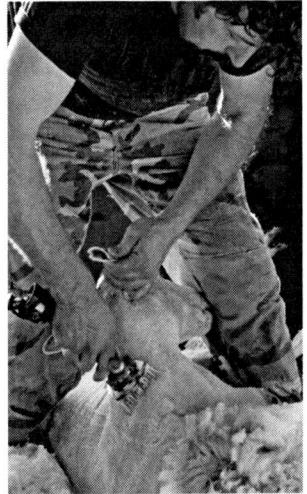

All types of sheep flock together to some extent, but some breeds tend to flock more tightly than others, especially when frightened. In addition, some breeds of sheep are flighty, meaning they panic or get upset easily. Very flighty sheep can be difficult for both humans and dogs to control. Sheep are generally pretty smart, but a panicked sheep is a stupid sheep. It can do unpredictable things, and it's easy to get yourself or your dogs hurt while working around them. The advantages of flighty breeds of sheep are that they tend to be both very hardy and good mothers, which are very desirable traits in sheep. For these reasons, people and dogs adjust to the ways of flighty breeds in order to have the advantages of their good traits.

Sheep that have been tamed through excessive handling by humans may not have the normal desire to flock. Extremely tame sheep, such as lambs that have to be bottle-fed or lambs that have been handled a lot by kids who raise for them 4-H projects, don't act like normal sheep in a number of ways, only one of which is their lack of flocking instinct. Not surprisingly, sheep that don't have the desire to flock also don't respond normally to being worked by a dog. They've lost their desire to seek safety in numbers, and they've also lost their ability to behave like prey when a dog approaches them. They'll often ignore a dog, acting like it's not even there. In addition, adult sheep that were bottle-fed as lambs can become very annoying to people as they grow up. They may jump up on you like they did as babies being fed, or they may feel no fear of you and butt you. At the very least, they tend to hang around at your feet and get in your way. You're very aware they're no longer little and cute, but unfortunately they are not.

Another situation that will cause a sheep to leave the safety of the flock is when a ewe is giving birth. If she has the space, she will normally separate herself from the others for a few hours before birth and may spend as long as a day or two away from the flock after giving birth. She

needs this time to bond with her babies and for her babies to recognize her as their mother.

A ewe can become very aggressive to dogs if they try to make her move right after she's lambed. However, due to bad weather or other circumstances, it's sometimes necessary to move a ewe and her babies back to the barn for a while. It takes a good dog to convey the attitude to the maternal ewe that it will not hurt her babies yet still convey the attitude of quiet authority that convinces the ewe to move.

Once the ewe has bonded with her babies, she will return to the flock. She may continue to show maternal instinct by being aggressive to the dogs, however. It takes just the right amount of pressure from the dog to move a flock of ewes with lambs. I've seen a ewe come busting out of the middle of the flock to butt a dog that's putting too much pressure on it by being too close or having too much of a threatening attitude.

My sheep are white-faced wool sheep. They're crossbred sheep—a mix of a calmer breed, Dorset, and a flighty breed, border cheviot. I try to keep a high percentage of the calmer Dorset in the cross. This mix gives me hardy sheep that are good mothers but not

as flighty and difficult to handle as purebred cheviots. My mostly Dorset crossbred sheep tend to be somewhat "heavy," needing a lot of push or pressure from a dog to move them. They're also not very reactive to people, making them easier to get close to and handle. It's a good compromise in both good and bad traits and these sheep do well in my area.

When I go to compete in sheepdog trials, the sheep are usually different breeds than my sheep here on the farm and consequently act differently. Because of this, I occasionally go to the farms of other people to get the competitive trial dogs used to working sheep different from ours at home. In general, dogs need to stay a great distance away from flighty breeds of sheep since they tend to be more reactive to a sheepdog's presence. A good dog will have enough natural "feel" for the sheep that it can tell roughly how far away it needs to be from a particular group of sheep when trying to go around or move them. However, in the sheepdog trial competitions, very precise control over the sheep is needed in order to make the obstacles required for the course. Both the dog and the handler need skill and experience on a lot of different kinds of sheep in order to be successful at the advanced levels. Sheepdog trials are meant to hone the skills of the dogs and handlers to a very fine art. I like to compete in them because it helps me to train my dogs to a high level and also to assess the strengths and weaknesses in each dog. In watching the best compete, it also helps me see what is possible for a great dog handler team to accomplish.

May was not yet a year and a half old when she competed in her first sheepdog trial. She no longer became carsick on trips and had been to a number of trials as a spectator by this point. In her first trial, she ran in the Pro/Novice class, where one of the team is a pro, and the other a novice or beginner. In our case, May was a less experienced dog with me as an experienced handler. The course in Pro/Novice is smaller and easier than the courses in the higher classes but can still be challenging for a beginner dog like May. She had been working very well at home but things can be quite different with the stress of a new place and new sheep. This trial was in Kentucky, over 400 miles away from our farm. The sheep were big blackfaced ewes that probably weighed 200-300 pounds compared to my sheep that weighed only 100-150 pounds. May had never seen sheep of this breed or sheep this big. I thought she could navigate the sheep around the trial course if things were easy and the sheep didn't get too wild. What I didn't know was whether she was mature enough to handle the sheep and listen to me at the same time if the situation started getting out of hand. It's one of those things you can't really know until the situation actually happens. To make things worse it was really windy, and I worried that May would have a hard time hearing me way out on the course. The outrun was about 250 yards to the sheep, which was pretty far away for May at a new field. This is the distance of two and a half football fields. The drive, the part of the course where the dog is supposed to take the sheep away from the handler and drive them in a straight line all the way through a set of panels, was not too long, maybe 75 yards. At the end of the short drive, May would have to bring the sheep back up to me and we would work together to try to put them into a pen.

As I walked out to the post where the handler must stand for most of the run, I made sure May saw, or "spotted" the sheep that seemed so far away. All of the sudden May seemed to me to be so young and small to be already competing on this size of a course with these strange, huge sheep. However, by hunkering down and staring intensely in the direction of the sheep, she signaled to me that she saw the sheep way out there and was ready to gather them. I sent her on her outrun on her good side, away to me. She ran out to the sheep as a good dog should—wide enough so that she didn't disturb the sheep but not so wide as to waste too much time or energy.

At the lift, or top of the outrun, when she was behind the sheep, she was a bit too close, making the sheep spurt off from the dog and person that were holding them in place. As the sheep ran toward me, with May in (too) close pursuit, I asked her to slow down, which would hopefully slow the sheep down. If May didn't try to slow the sheep down and control them soon, they would run harder and try to get away from her and we'd be in trouble. My fears that she wouldn't hear me as I tried to slow her down were for naught, as she and the sheep both slowed to a reasonable pace as they came closer to me.

May had them under good control when we worked together to turn them around the post where I was standing and she started driving them toward the first obstacle, a set of panels they would need to go through. The sheep are not supposed to go around the outside of the panels. If May could keep them on a straight line with my help, they would go right through the panels, the way they should. I was surprised and pleased that May held the line well and drove the sheep right through the panels.

Now all we had left to do to complete this beginner course was get the sheep back to me and into the pen. Once again, the sheep were running toward me, so I asked May to slow them down and she did. As they came toward me, I walked backwards to the pen, watching to make sure May was in control and brought the sheep straight to me. She had such good control of them by the time we got to the pen that they didn't even try very hard to go around it. Every way they went to try to break away from going into the pen, May was already there to stop them and together we convinced them to go into the pen.

There were 25 other dogs competing in her class, and May ended up tied for second place in the end. The areas where she'd lost the most points were at the lift where she was too close, causing the sheep to spurt off, and on the first part of the fetch, when the sheep were running too fast. Still, she had far exceeded my expectations of her in her first trial.

Taking May to the trial to work on different sheep helped intensify our partnership as well as helped me assess her strengths and weaknesses. Herding traits are a group of very complex behaviors, and it's hard to get a good balance of each trait in a dog. An example of one important trait that needs a good balance for the dog to be useful is the herding trait called eye. Showing eye is what makes a border collie's style of herding different from that of other herding breeds. When a border collie shows eye, it looks like it's stalking its prey, much like a cat getting ready to pounce on a mouse. This characteristic crouch and intense look intimidates livestock, and it's what makes them move away from border collies. However, it's not an all-or-nothing trait. Most working bred border collies have some degree of eye, but this trait is expressed in a range from what is called loose-eyed to strong-eyed. If a border collie is too loose-eyed it will have trouble controlling the sheep because it doesn't watch them intently enough. If a dog is too strong-eyed, it becomes so intense that it freezes and won't move, as if mesmerized by the sheep. Such strong-eyed dogs are called "sticky" because they tend to stick in

one place if they go eye-to-eye with the sheep, with neither the dog or the sheep moving. Some people like dogs with more eye or less eye than others. Sometimes the type of stock the dog will work dictates what amount of eye is best. But most people have a goal in breeding good working border collies that have a medium amount of eye. A dog with medium eye will be intense enough to watch the sheep closely and read what they're going to do yet not so intense that it stops all movement and won't let the sheep go anywhere when it needs to.

Another goal in breeding a useful dog is a balance between the dog wanting to push into the sheep to move them, and wanting to bunch the sheep together by constantly tucking in the sides of the group. If a dog only worries about keeping the sheep all together and tightly bunched, it may lose momentum and not move the sheep forward enough. If a dog only pushes in the middle of the group of sheep to keep them going without trying to keep the sides tucked in, it will leave sheep behind.

Working with lambs will often test if a dog has a good balance in the traits to both push and bunch. When a dog puts pressure on lambs, the lambs tend to try to double back instead of moving away the way adult sheep would. Lambs also tend to panic very easily. If the lambs are being worked without their moms, they have no leader and seem to not understand what to do. A dog must work very hard to both keep lambs together and keep them moving forward. May showed me early on that she was the best of my dogs at controlling and moving the lambs as a group. I had hit the jackpot on that balance of traits in May. She also had a medium amount of eye, so she was neither sticky nor too loose-eyed.

There are many other important areas that need a balance of traits, rather than extremes, for a dog to be as useful as it can be. There's a fine balance in reacting to the sheep while listening to and incorporating the wishes of the person. If the dog spends too much time reacting to the sheep and loses track of what you're asking it to do, the partnership is wrong. If the dog spends too much time listening for commands and doesn't think for itself about how to respond to the sheep, then the connection to the sheep is wrong. Every good breeding for working border collies is an effort to try to find the correct balance of traits to suit the person and the type of sheep the dog needs to work.

§§§

Carol and I were keeping contact by e-mail and phone. She told me many stories about Sky and how she was helping her. I found May was showing some of the same tendencies as Sky in wanting to comfort others. May's grandmother, Molly, was getting quite old and was having more and more trouble getting around. May would cuddle up to Molly and lick her tenderly on the face. Molly seemed to really enjoy this, even though to a person it would appear to be a bit too much "face time." May also paid her respects to the elderly Todd. He didn't like her to be in his face as much as Molly, but May would persist until he finally relented. At that point he would seem comforted by her.

May does not reserve her affection for the other dogs, however. She also loves to lie on the couch all cuddled up to family members, especially me. She doesn't mind invading our personal space, either. If I'm lying on the couch and she comes up to get a pet, she'll try to weasel her way right up under my chin, curling up in a little ball as she slithers her way up and against my chest to get where she wants to be. That girl could fit into a shoebox if she wanted to.

Even as she matured into an adult, May still enjoyed some puppy-like antics. Every night we had to have at least one incident of what I like to call the rolling growl. May would get on the rug in the den and roll around scratching her back, all the while play growling and moaning. This could go on for a long time. Sometimes she would stay on her back for a while afterward, upside down, feet in the air. If she had a long, thin, stick-like rawhide, she would lie on her back and hold one up between her front paws and chew on it. It looked like she was playing a flute.

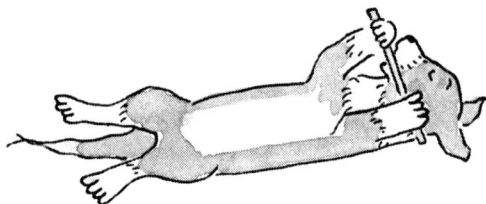

We were also entertained by the nightly flinging around of the stuffed raccoon. It squeaked too, which added to May's joy. The raccoon was flung from the couch to the floor to the other couch to the chair back to the floor and then made to squeal for a while before the routine started again. She never tired of it and neither did we.

Long before she ever competed in a sheepdog trial, May learned to enjoy the excitement of traveling with the competing dogs to the new farms where the trials are held. When we travel in my motor home, May gets to sleep on the bed with me. She's nice to sleep beside, except she's the only dog that's ever stolen my covers at night. In the middle of the night it's as if she suddenly wakes up and feels the need to bunch up the covers to make a fluffier bed for herself. She goes through this procedure of grabbing the covers in her mouth, jerking them all around to get more material to work with, then pawing and circling around for as long as it takes until the mound of covers are arranged more to her liking. Meanwhile, in my sleep, I slowly become aware I'm cold in certain places where the covers are now missing and that something is stomping on me.

Fortunately May makes up for the cover-stealing by being little and calm enough to be an excellent lap warmer when it's cold, while I'm sitting on the sidelines watching the other competitors run their dogs on the course with the sheep.

When the fall before her second birthday came, May needed to learn how to handle the ram used to breed the ewes. I don't keep rams year-round and she had not been old enough to work the ram the year before. Rams can be very aggressive, especially during breeding season. They're usually quick to let a dog know when it's too close or when they feel a bit cranky for no reason. This year I was using an older cheviot ram, who was quite cranky just on principal. I tried to introduce May to the ram slowly, but eventually she had to jump into the fire. Once, when I was letting the sheep through the gate, the ram got annoyed at how close May was and suddenly turned and butted her. I'm sure it wasn't pleasant for May, but she wasn't really hurt. Lots of dogs act brave until they get butted for the first time. Once they know they can get hurt, they don't want anything to do with confrontation and run off or won't work the offensive sheep. Some dogs decide they like the confrontation and pick more fights than they need to. Other dogs take it in stride and learn how not to get butted again while still standing up to the ram (or ewe) when needed. I certainly didn't want May to get butted, but I was very interested to see how she would react when it happened. She seemed surprised but not scared, which was good. She must've learned what she did wrong, because the ram didn't butt her again after that. One of the best ways to tell if a dog is doing the right thing is to watch how the sheep react to it. A person's idea of what's going on can be very subjective, but the sheep tell no lies.

At nearly two years of age, May was trained and had done at least a little of everything I needed her to do on the farm. She just needed time and experience to become the best that she could be at home. The question now was did she have what it takes to be a competitive dog at the highest level of sheepdog trials, the Open. There are plenty of good farm dogs, even excellent farm dogs, that don't have the "extra" it takes to be a top trial dog. Open trials on challenging courses with undogbroke sheep can push a dog to the limits of its ability. There's no way to tell if a dog can stand up to the challenge of high level competition except actually doing it.

I had taken May to a couple of sheepdog trials since her first one: she had done poorly at one and well at the other. However, she had more time, work, and experience under her belt since then, so I decided to run her in the Nursery class in the fall before she turned two. The Nursery class is for dogs under three years old during the qualifying year. The course is usually only a little less difficult than the Open course, so it's quite a challenge for a young dog. The outruns to the sheep are longer and the drive is more difficult than the Pro/Novice class May had been running in. Not all young sheepdogs are mature enough to run in the Nursery class, but I thought May could do it. So in the middle of October, I took her along to a trial where I had Mick and her mother, Kate, entered in Open. May was entered in three Nursery classes at this trial. If she placed in the top 20% in at least two of them, she would qualify for the National Nursery Finals.

Once again, May exceeded my expectations. She got second place in two of the three trials. This easily qualified her for the Finals. I would not be going to the Nursery Finals that next year, as it was in Oregon, over 3,000 miles away. However, it was very exciting that she had qualified so easily and early in the qualifying year.

May was a very exciting trial prospect. She seemed to enjoy the trials and learn something from each trial run. Most important, she usually kept a calm head about her and kept thinking of how to fix it when the sheep did things neither of us was expecting. Some dogs enjoy the competition just as people do, and rise to the occasion, delighting perhaps even themselves in their level of performance. May appeared to be one of those dogs.

9

§ Carol and Denise §

Do Border Collies Dream of Sheep?

Carol

Whether or not they are working, dogs' behavior and their view of the world are informed by the tasks they were bred to do. Nellie practices pointing by playing her special game. Other dogs guard the door, watch over the children the way Snowflake took care of me, or employ their inborn skills and instincts for work other than the job their breed usually does, like Sky.

A little less than two years after I brought Sky home from North Carolina, we were heading back to the farm where she was born for a visit. I tried to imagine Sky racing and playing with May, happy to be reunited. I tried *not* to think about the rest of the visit. I knew Denise would want to put Sky on sheep. I couldn't begin to imagine what would happen. Sky was a working dog, but her work was wildly different from the work border collies were bred to do. The only sheep she had seen since leaving the farm were the stuffed animals my friends kept buying for her. The last time she'd seen *real* sheep was when she was a tiny puppy, either peering out from Denise's jacket or standing on the ground for a few moments on the other side of the fence. I wondered what she'd think when she saw them. I wondered if, living in New York City, taking care of me, going to restaurants and riding in taxis, she dreamed of the sheep it was her heritage to work.

§§§

Denise

I often wondered how the pups from Kate's litter had turned out. Had I pegged them right, or had I missed the mark horribly as far as what they would be like as adults? Of course I was in contact with the owners but it wasn't the same as seeing them myself and comparing the adult with that same puppy I had studied so intensely for such a short period of time. I wondered especially about Sky, the pup who would need such strong nerves to live confidently in the big city and such a tremendous work ethic to do her job for Carol. Had I made the right choice?

Sky had stolen my heart from the beginning. She was so dainty, the smallest in the litter. She was sweet, yet fearless, and so in tune with me even before she could walk. I paid attention to her every move, her every sound, her every expression in each situation over the few weeks she was still Kate's, and mine. Early on I had an idea she might be the right pup for Carol. As Sky got older, she seemed to show even more of the traits that would enable her to work as a service dog. But pups can change as they grow up, sometimes dramatically. I checked my watch. It was time to leave for the airport. In a short while, I would see Sky again and find out if I had been right in choosing her for Carol.

As I drove to the airport, I felt strong emotions, just as I had nearly two years earlier when I drove Sky and Carol to the airport to say goodbye to Sky. I was excited and happy for her that she had such a wonderful home, and that she would lead such a fulfilling life. Still, it's always so very hard for me to let my puppies go. I cried when I kissed Sky good-bye, then stood watching Carol carry her through security and finally disappear on her way to the gate.

I recognized Carol in the distance at the airport and my eyes went immediately to Sky. As we approached each other, she acted as if she remembered me, but it could have been the way I acted that made it seem so. Clearly, I was drawn to her like a magnet. I surprised myself by bursting into tears. Sky jumped up and gave me a hug and kisses. I was immediately struck by how beautiful she was, my little dark tri, all grown up, and home again.

When we got back to the farm, we let Sky sniff around outside for a bit and then introduced her to May, cameras ready for the joyful greeting. But they weren't as happy to see each other as we thought they would be. They sniffed each other and acted as if they'd never met. They weren't people, after all. Who knows what they really thought or if they even remembered each other? At any rate, we were a little disappointed that their first meeting as adults was lukewarm at best.

Carol and I discussed trying Sky on the sheep for the first time. We decided it would be a good idea to put May in there with her, thinking they would naturally connect the way border collies working sheep together purely on instinct do. When we took Sky out to see the sheep from the other side of the fence, she was very interested in them. Her eyes lit up and she started barking as if to say, "Hey, I'm new here, but don't even think about messing with me." A pre-emptive strike, perhaps. Carol manned the camera while I took May and Sky in with the sheep. Sure enough, they each ran out on opposites sides and went around the sheep, crossing behind them and working together to hold the sheep to me. No matter which way I went, May and Sky worked with each other to bring the sheep to me.

Naturally, Sky was not as sure of herself as May, and continued to bark some. This is not unusual when border collies are first exposed to sheep and usually stops once they have more experience. Sky's tail was mostly down though, indicating she was serious and not just playing

with the sheep. After a short break for all of us to catch our breath, I took her back out to the sheep without May. Again, she instinctively knew to go to the opposite side of the sheep and bring them to me.

She worked and worked until her tongue was hanging way out and she was panting hard, even in the cold, but she still hadn't had enough of it. Sky had turned on to the sheep in a big way.

Afterward, Sky and May had a new understanding of each other. Their partnership working the sheep had helped them to become friends. At last, they romped and played in the yard together like they knew they were sisters.

When we all went back in the house, Sky would go to the doors leading to the back deck and whine, looking out into

the pasture for the sheep. Whenever we went outside, Sky would try to get under the fence to get to the sheep.

I just laughed, but Carol was worried we had created a monster! Would Sky now want to work sheep all the time and miss them once back in New York?

We worked Sky on the sheep a couple more times during the visit, both with and without May. Sky seemed to gain confidence each time she worked. It's always hard to tell how a dog would finish in its training by watching them in a few exposures to sheep, but I felt that she would have

made me a good little sheepdog had I kept her instead of May.

It was cold and raining for much of Carol and Sky's visit. When it was warm enough, we went for walks in the field, just as the dogs and I did most days. Sky seemed to enjoy the opportunity to stretch out and run with the other dogs and explore all the exciting farm sights and smells. After our walks, we'd curl up on the couch with a nice roaring fire in the fireplace, talking and watching the dogs play and interact. Sky was happy and independent while playing with the other dogs. When needed, she switched roles and donned her service dog cape to accompany Carol and me out to dinner each night. Wearing her cape, she was serious and quiet, attentive to Carol but not drawing any attention to herself. At the restaurant, the staff was amazed at how well-behaved Sky was. They were very interested in her, and finally, after we had eaten there several times, politely asked about her. Clearly, they had never seen a service dog at work. It was fascinating for me, too, to see this side of Sky, so very committed to Carol when needed, while being so much her own dog when "off duty."

As I watched and studied the adult Sky over the days she visited, I came to feel I had been right about my choice of the little dark tri for Carol. As Carol also came to know May, we felt that both sisters could have done either job. Though they'd been brought up in very different environments, they had turned out to be very much alike.

After the fun and excitement of Carol and Sky's visit, things returned to the normal farm routine. The ewes would lamb in spring. In early summer the lambs would be weaned and the ewe lambs destined to replace the older ewes would be chosen and kept. The other lambs were sold off. In the fall, the ram would go in to breed the ewes again and so the cycle went. There's a new generation of sheep each year on the farm. It's a frequent reminder of the natural cycle of life.

Sheep don't live nearly as long as people and neither do dogs. As much as we wish it wouldn't happen, dogs get old. Since I have a personal rule not to own more than six dogs at one time, and it's very rare for me to rehome an adult dog, it somehow worked out that I had mostly old dogs at this point. May was the only young dog I had. Kate, the next youngest, was going on seven years old when she had May's litter, and the spring after May turned two, Kate was nine. The others ranged up to nearly seventeen years old. I knew it would be a tough year as the older dogs, Molly and Todd, were reaching the end of their natural life spans. There was nothing really wrong with them but old age. Still, losing them was inevitable, and though we'd been through it before, it was hard to accept. All the love and good care in the world wouldn't make them young again. We would soon have to say our last goodbyes.

The others were still working but had been retired from sheepdog trial competition and would need to be relieved of most of their farm duties soon. As the older dogs began to wind down as was the way in the cycle of life and work on the farm, many responsibilities came to rest on the shoulders of a still-young May.

It was now time to stop wondering what May would be and start accepting what she was, both good and bad. Luckily she had ended up mostly good, but there are many things in working sheepdogs that are good in some situations and not in others. One of May's biggest strengths was her ability to focus and develop a plan while working sheep. This same strength became a fault when I needed her to do something different from what she thought, or when I needed her to change her focus quickly. Her focused commitment was part of who she was, and she was a good one overall in my estimation, so I just accepted each part of her without judgment. I was happy to have a sheepdog as talented as May to carry on the tradition here on the farm. Like her mother, Kate, her grandmother, Molly, and her great-grandmother, Micki, May had the dignity of purpose—important work and the feeling of fitting into an overall plan that she could understand. While it's impossible to know what's in a dog's soul, if she feels pride in a job well done, I think dogs do. I think May knows when she does her work well. She's not perfect—no dog is—but she's everything I could hope for as a funny, sweet house pet and a work partner on sheep.

§§§

Carol

If border collies dream of sheep, now Sky *really* had something to dream about.

But I wondered how she'd be when she got home. Would she miss the chance to do the work her sister did, her mother did, her grandmother did, and all the border collies in her family, all the way back to Scotland, had? Would she still want to be service dog? Would the life we had together still make her happy?

I didn't have long to wait to get my answers. By the time we got to the airport, Sky had slipped right back into her job. She seemed even more serious and more attentive than she'd been before our trip. In fact, shortly after we got home from North Carolina, she made another step up at the gym. When I used the whirlpool to warm up after my swim, I no longer hooked her leash to the wrought iron fence. One day, I just dropped the leash when I was ready to get into the whirlpool. She was on her own recognizance. She knew it and seemed very proud of herself, lying down right next to where I sat letting the jets of hot water take the aches out of my muscles. I don't know if anyone else noticed the difference, but I was really pleased.

Some border collie people think that putting a dog on sheep improves everything about the dog's life, that the chance to test drive some of the instincts inherited from their wolf ancestors helps the world make more sense to them. This seemed to be the case with Sky. After she'd worked alongside her sister and then on her own, gathering the sheep and bringing them to Denise, Sky seemed even more dedicated to her job than she'd been before. She took more initiative now. She seemed more mature, more self-reliant. She had become a better and more thoughtful partner. But despite having an absorbing job, lots of exercise, and a family who adored her, something was missing. She needed another dog to live with. There was just no way around it.

We decided to look for a rescue dog, a half-grown or adult dog who would be able to play hard with Sky from day one. Every few days I looked at Sweet Border Collie

Rescue on line, scrolling through all the pictures of dogs needing forever homes and reading their histories. But none of them grabbed me. I just wasn't ready.

Finally, in March, there he was, a nineteen-month-old border collie mix whose soulful eyes peered out at me from my computer screen and stole my heart.

We named him Monk, and from the moment he came to live with us, he and Sky were in sync. Once again, she had balance in her life, important work to do, a wonderful playmate and time to herself to rest, chew on a bone, or dream her own dreams.

Watching Sky when she slept next to me on the bed, her eyes moving beneath closed lids, her feet twitching, I wondered if she was back on the farm with May, circling the sheep, or if, instead, her dreams went farther back in time, to when her wild ancestors circled prey in order to survive, back to before the wolf became the dog.

Imagine life back then. There was no central heating, no doctor if you were sick or broke a bone, nothing much to do when you were bored. Worst of all, you never knew where you next meal was coming from, and you never knew if something large, fierce and hungry was hunting you.

Then, behold, a friend appeared.

His keen nose helped you find the prey you were after, and once you did, he prevented it from fleeing so that you could make the kill. When there was danger, he sounded an alarm, so you were less afraid. On cold nights, he lay tight against you, keeping you warm. He watched over the children. You had a helpmate now. You were connected.

As time went by, the humans provided food, shelter and eventually veterinary care, treats, and toys. The dogs took on a variety of roles, assistant to the hunter, help for the farmer, leader of the blind, protector of our homes. They learned to perfect and practice the jobs we bred them to do as well as those they discerned on their own. And so, thousands and thousands of years after that first mild-tempered wolf accepted a bone from one of our hirsute ancestors, May and Sky are doing what their forebears did, working alongside their human partners, each species contributing what it can for the survival and well being of both.

Lightning Source UK Ltd.
Milton Keynes UK
UKOW021224061211

183293UK00011B/133/P